BY THE HAIR OF MY CHIN

ISBN: 978-1-3999-0844-3

Printed by Book Printing UK
Remus House, Coltsfoot Drive, Peterborough, PE2 9BF

Foreword

Compared with today, my generation, like early Polaroid films, were late developers. Even when we had reached the age of eighteen, most of us would have defined the word sex as the bags that posh people had their coal delivered in. Ask us about national spirit or national butter, however, and we would at once wax eloquent - you see, we had had more serious, more important things to think about. Then ask us about National Service and we would have the floor to ourselves, as it's almost sixty years since its unmourned corpse was laid to rest. It's no coincidence that the last conscripts were just restoring themselves to civilisation at about the same time as the death penalty was abolished. Of course defence strategy, defence cuts and peacetime prosperity necessitated massive cuts in the armed forces, but changing attitudes also played their part. In a less authoritarian society it becomes more and more difficult to impose and justify conscription, and the welfare state could put the money involved to much better use. People still say that all the present youth of today need is a good dose of national service to straighten them out but they're wrong. It was not a civilising influence, rather the opposite, but it made boys into men at a time when a man must fight for his country when he was eighteen but yet could not vote for the government that sent him into battle until he officially achieved adulthood at twenty-one.

My national service was deferred for seven months while I took university entrance examinations and, importantly as it turned out, secured a place at university before being called up. During those seven months, with the suspended sentence hanging over me, I was able to observe school friends who preceded me into the forces, rarely getting a favourable reaction from them about their experiences. I also learned that every single one of my four closest friends at school during the war had avoided conscription. No wonder a certain amount of apprehension, perhaps even resentment, built up inside me. On the credit side, the headmaster at the school where I was so enjoying myself was an ex-Wing Commander and I thought I wouldn't mind being a part of the RAF which, because of its wartime exploits, had become top dog among the three services.

1. RUDE AWAKENINGS

One morning in 1950, just as spring was beginning to oust winter from its icy perch, an official-looking buff envelope arrived for me in the morning post. It invited me, nay *commanded* me, to attend a medical examination in Norwich to discover whether or not I was fit for National Service. Just for a moment I cherished a hope that something would crop up to disqualify me from entry but there was a dilemma there. As a person who enjoyed a variety of sports and who, through playing games regularly, was more than passably fit, I would not have wanted to tell people that I was medically unfit for the armed forces, nor would I have liked to have had a physical defect that classified me below A1. It was thus with strangely mixed feelings that I waited to keep that appointment.

With a mixture of expectation and foreboding, I walked briskly down to the recruiting centre on the appointed morning. As I turned into the gateway, a young farmworker dropped in beside me. He had on a well-worn pair of dungarees which were liberally coated with pig manure, his wellington boots were similarly smeared. Beneath his swill-spattered beret he wore a broad grin.

"Good morning," I greeted him.

"Morn'n," he replied.

"Looking forward to this lot?" I asked.

"Not bothered, really. Don't s'pose they'll ’ave me anyway."

Before I had time to pursue the matter we were being shepherded into the medical inspection area. Having stripped off, as instructed, a bottle was thrust into our hands, into which we were required to drain off a sample; having been well trained to see to such things before going out into strange company, it was some time before I could oblige. My neighbour in the next cubicle was in even more difficulty and while we waited patiently, he related the well-worn story of a youth in similar circumstances: unable to deliver, he had asked his neighbour to do the necessary for him and they were both rejected as diabetics.

We moved on to have our reflexes tested by a little gnome of a doctor. Having told me to cross one knee on top of the other, he produced a small rubber hammer with which he smote me firmly below the left knee-cap. My foot jerked smartly upwards and with unsuspected agility, the ageing doctor took sufficient evasive action just to avoid being kicked under the chin. Looking up with a broad grin on his face he uttered one of the catch-phrases of the moment-

"That was a good one was it not?" he chuckled, before passing me on to have my ears tested.

There, an even more decrepit-looking man, wielding a mobile searchlight, peered owl-like into my ears, though I doubt if he could really see much - or hear a great deal for that matter. He seemed very satisfied with what he saw and so it was with all those who examined me. Although we were secretly pleased to be told that we were fighting fit, we nonetheless felt that it was something of a conspiracy to be examined by such a bunch of superannuated physicians.

The next step was an intelligence test in which the opening question was to pick out from a list of five words on the right of the paper a word that was roughly opposite to one printed on the left; the first two went roughly like this.

HEAVY is the opposite of:

(a) TOMORROW

(b) WHITE

(c) OCTOPUS

(d) LIGHT

(e) NOISILY.

START is the opposite of:

(a) THURSDAY

(b) BLANKET

(c) EXTRAORDINARY

(d) PEPPERMINT

(e) STOP.

We moved on to mechanical aptitude tests and a few simple sums.

Keep an eye on the farm-worker. During each of these written tests he has sat patiently looking out of the window, with his arms folded; at the conclusion of each paper he has been approached by the invigilator to explain his in-activity. Has he not understood the instructions, or was the paper too difficult? No, he explains, it is far simpler than that - he cannot read or write. The reason no one at the recruiting centre knew of this was because no one asked. Even so he must sign the question paper at the bottom, which he does with a cross, under which the invigilator scribbles an explanation for the marker's benefit.

Thus it was for all the written tests, following which we were interviewed by an officer from the branch of the armed forces we would prefer to join. The navy was not taking anyone at this time, because they did not think they could train a person over a period of eighteen months to be of any use to them. You could join the navy but you had to commit yourself for more than the compulsory national service engagement. Effectively, then, the choice was RAF, Army, RAF Regiment or Pioneer Corps. I had to explain my reasons for opting for the RAF. Firstly, my father had been in the Royal Flying Corps at the end of the First World War, and I told them that. Secondly, I had heard such dire reports from my friends of what it was like in the army that there really seemed to be only one sensible choice; I did not tell them that. In the event, I was glad that the RAF accepted me because, after the period of basic training, there was certainly not the same rigid check on your liberty as there seemed to be in the army.

Still smiling, the farmworker, leaving in his wake the aroma of an overripe stilton cheese, was whisked briskly from the RAF officer, who felt sure the man was much better suited to the army, to the army officer who recommended him for the Pioneer Corps. After the briefest of interviews, the Pioneer Corps said they were very full and, much as they hated to disappoint him, they felt he would be far better off on the farm. The smile disappeared. Though he actually said nothing by way of protest, he forced disappointment through every pore of his now saddened face. They were adamant, however, in rejecting him for national service, consoling him that he was doing just as important a job on the land, piloting his tractor and shovelling his muck to keep the nation's larder full. Still leaving heavily larded footprints, he walked dejectedly away.

The rest of us were told whether or not we had secured our first choices and were advised of our imminent call-up, before finally being dismissed. Although we were not yet in their clutches, there was an unmistakable feeling that the process had begun. There was an air of forced friendliness which left us in no doubt of the fireworks to come. We left the building in subdued mood, crossing the yard in gloomy silence. At once the air was rent with the noise of a powerful motorcycle bursting into life, somewhere round the corner just out of view. As it burst into sight we saw that it was ridden by our farm-worker. Slowing as he approached us, his beaming smile in full blossom, he gave us a huge wink, revved up and was gone!

Walking back to school for lunch that day I found it strangely comforting to know that someone had beaten the system, for that, undoubtedly, was what the farm-worker had done despite overplaying his hand. Certainly, anybody who was prepared to go to such lengths deserved his prize, because he would have made a good dispatch-rider in the army and the final, farewell wink had left us believing that his feigned illiteracy would not have withstood the test of a more thorough investigation. For me, however, a few more blissful days remained before the rudest of rude awakenings.

I had definitely not had the ideal preparation for the cold shower of national service for, as the Senior Citizen at school, I had been subjected to very few curbs. There was a spirit of friendliness and cooperation amongst both staff and pupils. It was accepted, for instance, that with food still rationed, boys were often hungry after their day's quota of school food. After supper in the evening, two senior boys would slip quietly round to the local fish and chip emporium to buy numerous portions of supplementary rations. The duty masters knew about it but never interfered because the privilege was never abused. One master, a particular friend, used to turn a blind eye but insisted that I should not allow smoking in return. Frequently, in the late evening, we would chat over a cup of coffee with the conversation always coming round to horse-racing. One thing he could not advise me about was national service because he had not been required to do it; I was most fortunate to have a friend in the village at home to give me much needed counsel.

Ben had been in the Royal Navy during the war, serving most of his time afloat on cruisers. It was he who advised me of the harsh realities of service life for which, he realised, I was totally unprepared. He told me of a friend he had made on one occasion who borrowed five pounds from him one weekend, a good deal of money for a rating to lend. What he did not know until too late was that the 'friend' had been posted to a far distant place and he was never to see him again. First lesson, then: neither a borrower nor a lender be. Next, however stupid or unreasonable an order may seem, obey it without question, without, of course, breaking the law or service rules. Most importantly, never trust anyone.

This last I found unacceptable, since my whole life at home and at school was based on people trusting me and me them. Nevertheless, he would never tire of impressing this upon me. As if to underline the importance of the message he lent me the combination lock and bar that he had used on his kit-bag in the navy. His strict instructions were to keep my possessions securely locked away and never to leave money or valuables in my pockets while I was asleep during the night. His advice with regard to money was to tuck my wallet inside the pillow after lights out. I was not inclined to heed his words, but they were quickly to be proved true.

Amid kind words and sincere regrets, I left school on a Friday. The next day we had a party to celebrate my sister's twenty-first birthday, with goodwill and good food abounding. A final fling for me, because, on the following day, Sunday, I had to report to Padgate. I am certain that no three days of my life have ever contained such contrasts, and as the train carried me north I reflected upon the drastic downturn my life was taking. I made up my mind that, once my basic training was over, I would not allow national service to affect my normal life at home. I know now that I was very naïve, and this is what Ben had seen. That I did not drink, smoke or swear must have made me rather boring to most and made me the loner that it suited me to become.

2. WELCOME

Padgate. Number One Reception Unit. Mary Tudor would not even have remembered Calais if she had known the hell-hole that was Padgate. On a wet, cheerless Sunday afternoon there could be few more depressing places. Inquisitive heads peered out of squalid huts, accompanied by the familiar shouts of- "You'll be sorry." Until the moment of arrival at this drab prison I had still nursed fading hopes that the RAF of 1940, with the "jolly good show," and "Whizzo," image, might still be lurking in the wings. But no, "you'll be sorry" was the reality which it never ceased to live up to. Understandably, perhaps, for the permanent staff who were required to deal with us, we were another load of refuse tipped on their doorstep, to be processed as roughly and as grudgingly as possible. The word 'welcome' had long since been deleted from their vocabulary as they bundled us around like so many cattle.

We reported to some disinterested pen-pusher that we had arrived and were shown to our temporary quarters. There is nothing positive to be said about them, so my sole comment would be that, to my surprise and relief, there weren't any fleas. I do not know why, but I had imagined that fleas and bed bugs would be in permanent residence, and thankfully I was wrong. I picked out a bed, set my case beside it and pondered Ben's words: "Don't trust anyone." The bunch that I had been herded with were as unremarkable as I was and equally despondent. I decided to have a wash, following my sooty train journey. After rummaging in my case for the splendid new bath towel which my mother had packed for me, I made my way to the wash room at the back of the hut.

It was deserted as I entered, to see a row of wash-basins down one side, and a central gangway with a row of lavatories on the other side. At head height on the division between each of these lavatories was a clothes peg. I stress that, as I removed my jacket and hung it, together with my new towel, on a peg somewhere in the centre of the building, there was no one else in sight.

With my back to the peg, but with me looking at a shaving mirror, I soaped my face and had a brisk wash, finishing with a rinse in cold water. Turning to clutch my new towel to dry my face, I found myself grabbing my jacket instead. My eyes now wide open, I could see only too clearly that my towel had gone. I had neither heard nor seen anyone, but my towel, boldly marked as it was with a Cash's name tape, had disappeared. To this day I can offer no satisfactory explanation; my only thought was that someone had secreted himself in one of the lavatories and had stolen the towel at the moment when I was soaping my face. I never saw the towel again. My report to the rather evil looking sergeant in charge was met with stony indifference tinged with disbelief. If I wasn't careful, I would get myself an early reputation as a trouble-maker.

Back in the billet, my inquiries about the possibility of anyone having seen the towel were met either with blank faces or indignant replies of: "I hope you're not accusing me." Well, of course I wasn't, but as I got a smaller towel from my case, I finally realised that what Ben had been trying to warn me of had to be heeded. In a very short while the wisdom of his words was to be painfully underlined for some of the others in the billet. I was thankful that my jacket hadn't been stolen, although I could not understand why.

I flopped down on to my bed pondering miserably how my fortunes had changed in just twenty-four hours. Why, only yesterday I had been enjoying a family party and now this.

My broodings were interrupted by my first acquaintance with a soon-to-be familiar cry:

"Get outside!"

We shuffled out in dribs and drabs and were loosely arranged in some sort of formation. The sergeant addressed us in officious tones: -

"Blood donors, that's what we want. Blood donors to give a pint of blood in the morning. Forty of 'em. It don't hurt and it don't take long but we got to have forty blood donors. All those volunteering to give a pint of blood take one pace forward."

Eighteen people stepped forward, which was obviously displeasing to the sergeant, for he then went on: -

"I think I should warn all you others what hasn't moved that if you fail to volunteer you will be on cook-house fatigues at six o'clock in the morning. Not a very pleasant prospect, especially in your civilian clothes, so let's have no more nonsense. Are there any more who wish to volunteer?"

To their eternal credit, all but a handful of those who had stepped forward in the first instance now stepped back into line. No new volunteers offered their services and so the sergeant had only six instead of his original eighteen. I was immediately reminded of Ben's fourth maxim - never volunteer for anything. The point about this particular incident was that, if someone had explained to us the importance of giving blood, in pleasant terms, we would all have willingly volunteered. To be threatened as we were alienated us permanently. The sergeant, however, was true to his word and I for one was marched off to the cookhouse at six the next morning.

I remember writing a letter home telling of the experiences of my first few hours and apologising for losing the towel. I also expressed doubts about whether my case and civilian clothes would ever reach home. I had been told that, once we had been fitted for uniforms and fully kitted out, we would not be allowed to keep the clothes that we had brought with us. The cases would be parcelled and labelled to be sent on to our homes. In view of the immediate loss of my towel, I imagined that the rest of my stuff would go the same way. Remarkably, it eventually arrived home intact. My letter posted, I turned in early for the night, some time before lights out at ten o'clock. Although there were only three pounds in my wallet, I was at great pains to tuck it inside my pillow without anyone seeing. In a way, losing the towel was a blessing in disguise, because it made me extremely careful about my belongings for the whole of my national service.

Perhaps I should have shared my thoughts about keeping money away from thieving hands, but I was tired and thinking of my early morning appointment. In the event, I was probably wise to stay silent, because it might have cast suspicion on me.

When I got back from the cookhouse fatigue the billet was in turmoil. Seven of the occupants had had their money stolen overnight. We were all made to stand by our beds and turn out our pockets. Every one of us was under suspicion, which made us uneasy of each other's company for the few days we remained together. The sergeant then addressed us in contemptuous tones before storming back to his quarters. We were easy prey, of course, and more than ever discouraged by this latest turn of events when we had still not been on the camp for twenty-four hours. It came as no surprise to me to learn a couple of days later that it was the sergeant who had stolen the money. He was caught red-handed doing the same thing in another reception billet.

There was an air of unreality as we were initiated into our new surroundings.

The main objective was to get us documented and fully kitted with RAF issue clothes.

The acquiring of kit bordered on the farcical. The first requirement was a kit-bag, on which we stencilled the equally essential service number. We then made our way to a hangar-like building with racks of clothing fronted by long counters. Instantly categorised by those issuing the kit behind the counters, we were thrown large, medium or small vests, socks, shirts and so on. The shirts were a particular abomination of coarse material with detachable collars. A curiosity among the issued kit and a constant source of tired jokes from the NCO supervising was ‘the housewife’. It was a small cotton envelope containing needles and thread and wool for us to be able to sew on buttons and mend our socks.

"Never thought you'd 'ave an ‘ousewife to keep you company, did you?" He quipped.

Or, "Don't let your 'ousewife give you the needle, will you?"

Such gems of wit put us in good humour for the fitting of uniforms and overcoats. Most of the tunics and trousers were second-hand; my “best blue” jacket was like a patchwork quilt, with a nonmatching square of material at the bottom of the left-hand overlap about an inch longer than the right. Because I was particularly long in the arm, my battle dress tunic was always tight, but it was the best they could do, and they would brook no argument. One or two of the short ones in our billet did manage to get their trousers changed because they were far too long. My own special problem was boots. I take a size twelve which, at the time, was considered to be ridiculous. One pair of best boots and one pair of square-bashers were issued to each new recruit but they did not have any to fit me. They did, however, have a pair of black shoes in my size for my immediate use and the next day a quite comfortable pair of best boots came to light, but no square-bashers, with all those dreadful studs in. It was over a month before I finally received those boots, and they were to be a source of great amusement for the flight sergeant at my basic training camp. In the meantime, I was marching in very cosy, noiseless footwear. I didn't mind having my leg pulled about the boots, especially after I had travelled home on the Thursday of that first week for the Easter weekend.

Travelling across country from the north west of England to Norwich was a tediously slow business involving several changes. It must have been midnight when I boarded a carriage at Ely (or was it March?) for the penultimate lap of the journey. There was just one other occupant of the compartment, also a new recruit in the RAF. He was taller than me (I was 6ft 2) and lived in Norwich, where his mother was a schoolmistress. Sitting on opposite sides of the carriage, we chatted for a while before putting our feet up to go to sleep. I was woken by the train lurching to a halt in the station where we had to change. Opening my eyes, I was confronted by the soles of this huge pair of boots. My travelling companion was still asleep as I contemplated his enormous feet. I woke him and, unable to curb my curiosity, I enquired as to the exact size of his footwear.

"Size fourteen," he replied.

"Fourteen!" I exclaimed with a note of triumph in my voice, and ever after that I was not in the least self-conscious about my size twelves. The funny thing was that they had his size fourteen in stock!

The overcoat was the one really good thing with which I was issued. Snug fitting, extremely warm, it was to give me very good service indeed. For some reason the overcoat was treated separately from the rest of the issue, it being pointed out that if we ever lost it, we were liable to court-martial! I never did discover whether this was just another of those many idle threats with which we were plagued throughout our training period, but they seemed to be in earnest about it.

While I was getting my overcoat, I fell into conversation with a diminutive north-country youth who had been at Padgate for just over three weeks. He had been ill on arrival and had not recovered fitness in time to move on with his original intake. Accordingly, he had been put to work in the clothing stores, which suited him admirably. Why he confided in me I shall never know, but it began with me mentioning the awful shirts with which I had just been issued. He offered to exchange them for me and, true to his word, he brought me some much better-quality shirts which I think were officer issue. On my first trip home I bought some Van Heusen collars to match them so that my shirts, at least, were respectable.

We sat in the mess at lunch and found that he lived very close to the town in Lancashire to which my family had moved during the war. In the course of conversation, he told me how his father ran a men's outfitting shop and what a stroke of good fortune it had been to be put into the clothing store. Two or three times each week as the opportunity presented itself, he sent his father a parcel of the best quality shirts, socks and so on for which there was a brisk sale in the family shop. He had just heard, however, that he had at last been re-flighted and would not be able to send his father any more supplies. Lucky for him, I thought, that the temptation had been removed, because goodness knows what would have happened to him had he been caught.

It had become a source of increasing alarm that we might actually be posted to Padgate to do our square-bashing, especially as we were regaled by inmates of new recruits breaking under the strain: -

"My mate drank half a bottle of Dettol," was one of the stories that went the rounds, "and when he got over it and was told he had to go back, he swallowed another half a bottle." How true it was we never found out, but it sounded quite plausible at the time, and it did nothing for our peace of mind. We had to go through the mill and, presumably, one place was no better or worse than another to be ground down, but at the time trivial things assumed monumental importance and could be most upsetting for those of a nervous disposition. One such person had supposedly thrown himself off the water tower a week earlier, rather than face any longer the rigours of Padgate. Unlike the Dettol drinker, he had not survived. That, we were assured, was definitely true.

"Morrison – West Kirby," I heard with relief. So it was not to be the dreaded Padgate after all. Later I was able to see the funny side of actually being pleased to be sent to West Kirby, even though I had not the slightest idea of where it was or what it was like. With kit-bag brimming full I made my way to Warrington station after a four day stay at Padgate that had seemed like at least as many weeks and, almost light-heartedly, waited for the train that I was sure was taking me to better things.

3. FINDING MY FEET

By far the most pleasant thing about arriving at West Kirby on that Wednesday afternoon was the knowledge that we would be leaving for the Easter break on the following day. Our kit bags were bundled into lorries to be carried on ahead of us while we marched the mile or so from the station to the camp. It was more shambling than marching, but it gave our future drill instructors an opportunity to show off the power of their lungs and the weakness of their vocabulary. The first, sharp, impression of the camp was of a bleak, wired-in compound, more fitted for the incarceration of criminals than for the training of young recruits.

Once locked in, we were to be threatened, bullied, and run off our feet so as not to be given time to work out a defensive strategy. We had no rights and we were useless; guilty until proven innocent and an affront to the regular Air Force. A dissenting voice was a troublemaker and therefore likely to find himself in trouble, big trouble. How else could a numerically small team of seasoned instructors cope with successive waves of cooped up youths? Theirs was not an easy job, requiring them, as it did, to make themselves deliberately disliked. Partly because, if they were in any way friendly towards us, they would find it difficult to impose strict discipline, and partly to promote teamwork within each flight of men who would be united in at least one thing – dislike of their instructor. In addition, it is doubtful if a really popular NCO could have lasted as a drill instructor.

Our kit bags had been dumped in an open-ended, hangar-like building at the bottom of the camp. Several corporals stood by this huge pile, picked up the nearest bag, yelled out the number on it and then hurled it in our direction. In the noise and confusion, all staged for our benefit, it was difficult to hear what was being said, so that the majority of the kit bags thudded to the ground. At the top of each bag was a china drinking mug and many of these perished in the melee. It was a depressing spectacle, not least for the way it seemed to amuse our instructors, who then shepherded us to our living accommodation.

'Home' for the next nine weeks was a grim, low-roofed, brick building, not dissimilar in appearance to a small battery-hen house. Here, twenty-five recruits lived, or more correctly, existed, under the perpetual scrutiny of their instructor corporal, who had his own separate room at the top end of the hut. Each one of us was responsible for his own bed and the bed-space to the right of it. Every morning the twelve beds at either side of the hut had to be lined up with a piece of string. Mattresses were folded back with blankets and sheets folded in a neat pile on top. A clean towel was laid across the bare springs at the bottom of the bed with knife, fork, spoon and drinking mug arranged as a place setting in the middle. All these, in turn, had to be lined up straight. Bed spaces must be swept and polished.

The rest of the hut - the centre gangway, the windows and so on - was taken care of by the regular 'bull nights' which were spent cleaning, polishing, scrubbing and whitening where necessary. The very first of these extraordinary affairs has remained clearly in my memory. In the frenzied, uncoordinated activity there was something of the panic that seizes an overturned ants' nest, with people rushing this way and that as the corporal shouted his orders and expressed his general dissatisfaction with each completed task. We would never win the prize at this rate. Prize? What prize? There was no end to our good fortune because the smartest of the four huts in our group would be awarded the one radio available, to use for a week until the next judgement day. He prided himself on the smartness of his hut and if we did not win, then heaven help us. Imagine our relief and elation when we were adjudged the winners for the first week. What we did not know was that the 'system' dictated that each hut won the radio in turn, though not necessarily in strict ABCD order, so for the following three weeks we were urged to greater effort until our turn came round again, by which time we did not really care whether we had the radio or not. It says a good deal for the powers of persuasion of our instructors that they were able to goad us, week after week, into striving for such a ludicrous reward.

It would have been some time after eight in the evening when the hut was pronounced fit for inspection, by which time we were all ready for refreshment. There was time for a quick trip to the NAAFI. A fellow sufferer, a cockney as a matter of fact, came over to me to enquire: -

"Coming down to the NAAFI for a firkin, mate?"

Now I had just completed my university entrance and straight to my mind came a quotation about a 'firkin of moist and corny ale.' So my reply went: -

"You mean a firkin of moist and corny ale, don't you? Sounds all right."

"Nah," he scorned, "I just meant a firkin cup o' tea."

My disillusionment was complete.

There are so many things about which, with hindsight, we say, "If only we'd known at the time," and none more so than with all the greenness we showed during our square-bashing. We must have seemed heaven-sent to our hard-boiled instructors, who showed no mercy in exploiting us. And why shouldn't they, with such an exacting and exhausting job? Their richest pickings were, in fact, in the spit and polish stakes and we were not alive to it until it was all over. Every recruit had to blanco his large and small packs, his webbing and gaiters, using a grey, sludgy liquid for the purpose. At an early stage, the billet corporal would appear during a blancoing session full of good advice. Best of all, he knew where he could purchase blanco in bulk much more cheaply than we could get it. With threat and promise equally mixed, he told us of the neat arrangement whereby, for sixpence a week from each of us, he could buy blanco by the barrel. Good idea lads? Right, let's have your first sixpences now and it's a deal. We paid up like lambs and he kept to his side of the bargain by keeping us regularly supplied with blanco that he got for nothing from the stores. That was only the beginning of the 'bargains' he could get his hands on.

Brasso and Duraglit were two more commodities in which he had virtually cornered the market. Another sixpence apiece and we were on to another good thing, while stocks lasted. And think of all the black boot polish we would need. Guess what? He had some at a ridiculous price. How did another sixpence each sound for the bargain of the year? Bet we'd never thought of brown boot polish, had we? Well, no, we hadn't. Silly, because that was the only thing to bring the stocks of our rifles up to the required standard and, boy! Would they look good? Had we thought, however, about the brown polish rubbing off on our grey-blue uniforms? Do you know, we hadn't even considered it? Methylated spirits was the thing for that and we would have the smartest rifles in the whole of Cheshire. Well, we couldn't miss out on that one, could we? Not for a mere sixpence. It was never-ending but the crowning gem was still to come. Trousers needed pressing constantly, and shirts had to be ironed when we were not allowed off the camp? (He had waited for this until after we returned from the Easter break.) Our luck was in, though, because, by one of those inexplicable strokes of good fortune, our corporal, our very own knight of the bull-night, had a spare iron, pretty well a new one at that. Irons were expensive things but even so, it was a steal at twenty-five shillings. Good gracious! How extraordinary that it should be that price, because that worked out at exactly a shilling each.

And so we acquired a communal iron which was pressed into constant use! There was, inevitably perhaps, a lovely tailpiece to this particular rip-off. Just before we were due to leave West Kirby, our philanthropic corporal dropped a few well-aimed hints. It was customary to give the hard-working DI, who had knocked us into such splendid shape, (and wasn't he proud of us?), a farewell gift. We had very little, if any, spare cash so would it not be a good idea to give him, say, the iron? After all, we couldn't split it into twenty-five and each take a piece, so, how about it? Good idea. We gave him the iron - which he could then sell again, for the umpteenth time, to the next entry. He really had to be admired for his cheek and his tenacity, but we were so pleased to be rid of him and of West Kirby that we really didn't mind. Who says there were no supplementary benefits in those days?

The silk purse, they say, never derives from the sow's ear, but I suppose our billet was in as good a shape as could reasonably have been expected, and it was the people in it, after all, who made it a tolerable living place. It needed a few characters and it had them. One, a very smooth, well-spoken young man who regularly asserted his independence and individuality but somehow, with a mixture of charm and guile, always got away with his indiscretions. He was a good games player and, at the very moment when any NCO appeared to have him in a corner, he would be whisked off to represent the RAF at some sport or other and escape the noose. His prime asset as far as we were concerned was his gift for mimicry. He could make himself sound and look uncannily like our billet corporal. At the end of a day when the corporal had been particularly tiresome, we would urge our champion to do his party piece. Though I could never really understand why we should want yet another dose of that harsh, grating voice. One evening he got up on a chair, pulled his beret severely down over his right eye and launched into one of his brilliant tirades.

"If you don't swing those flaming arms, I'll cut them orf at the elbows and beat you to death with the soggy ends." It sounded funny coming from him and as he warmed to his task there was an increasing crescendo of noise and laughter. Now in full flow he, and for that matter all the rest of us, failed to see or hear the corporal make a, for once, stealthy entry from the other end of the hut. We were just hearing the oft-repeated bit about the doubtful parentage when a shattering yell had us all jumping in the air.

"Get off that chair and report to me in the morning, laddie, after breakfast. As for the rest of you, you're all as bad as he is, and I won't forget this in a hurry. I'll make your lives so miserable you'll wish you'd never been born." We felt sure he meant it, but we were much more concerned about what would happen to our mimic. We need not have worried because, at seven the next morning, wearing his best blue, he bid us all good day as he was off to somewhere down south for the next few days to play for the RAF. He had wisely refrained from telling the corporal and was clear of the camp before the latter found out that his bird had flown. With so much happening each day and with, no doubt, a warning of hands off from the appropriate officer, the matter was forgotten and no further action was taken. The charmed life continued for our sporting hero, whose luck even extended to his permanent posting. Sailing was one of his accomplishments and he had requested to be stationed at Southampton Water. And that is exactly where he was sent.

The other remarkable character was of a totally different nature. Life had to proceed at his pace and on his terms and nobody would upset the pattern, least of all some over-rated corporal. All right, if the corporal wished to rise at six-thirty, and all the others in the billet with him, that was their choice. He could be yelled at and threatened but not until around a quarter to eight was he prepared to emerge. By this time, everyone else was back from breakfast, tidying their belongings and the billet in general. Off went our eccentric friend for his breakfast. His bed and bed space, untidied as they always were, made it impossible for our side of the room to line up anything until he came back. He would stroll unhurriedly in and immediately reproach me.

"Look at the mess my bed is in. Do you mean to say that you couldn't just fold up my blankets for me and sweep my bed space?

Fine pal you turn out to be. What are mates for, I should like to know? We're all in this together, you know."

At first I used to think he was joking, but not a bit of it. There was more to come.

"Oh no! My boots are filthy. Surely you could have put a bit of polish on them when you were doing yours, or is that too much trouble for you?"

"I did my boots last night while you were flopped out on your bed all evening," I would begin.

"All the more time you had to do mine this morning then," he would interrupt.

Because he had put us so far behind, we would rally round in our own interest, but more and more we left him to his own devices. He never altered and he always managed to avoid serious trouble. Unfortunately, he became isolated, since he seemed to take the whole lot of us for fools. Every so often during the day, the instructing corporal would give a ten-minute break for a smoke. I always used to stuff a daily paper in a pocket or somewhere, to read while the others were smoking. This chap never took any cigarettes with him during the day. His method was to see what brands people were smoking and borrow one of the expensive cigarettes until the evening. During the day he would borrow seven or eight and then, in the evening, he would buy the cheapest cigarettes available from the NAAFI to pay back all the lenders. He probably became a millionaire entrepreneur.

To the raucous cry of- "Get outside," we began each morning by assembling outside the billet to await instructions for the day.

Whatever they were they always included drill, weapon training and P.T. For almost everybody, early problems with marching or saluting were quickly overcome but there was one person in our group who could not master the art of marching; however hard he tried, he could not prevent himself from marching with the same arm and leg going forward together. I seemed fated to be placed either in front of or behind him, so that I either kicked the back out of his footwear or he battered mine. Eventually, as we neared our final stages, he did not come on parade and on inspection day he looked after the billet.

Whenever we returned from P.T. it was compulsory for us to take a shower and, before we had experienced the scramble that it produced, it was something to look forward to. After one attempt, however, it proved to be yet another penance. We would be marched back to our quarters, there to be dismissed for a shower. We rushed to our beds for a towel and tore back to the showers opposite, trying to get ourselves to the front of the queue. There were ninety-eight people to share eight showers. No problem, you might think, and you would have been right had there been a half an hour available to carry out the exercise. But there wasn't. After no more than ninety seconds, the corporal began to bellow- "Get outside!" On that first occasion, we were sure he had made a mistake for, obviously, the lucky eight at the head of the queue were still showering. We thus took absolutely no notice of the repeated warning for us to get outside. In no time at all, the door was ripped open to reveal a crimson-faced corporal, apparently about to explode.

"You lot got clorf ears?" he inquired, not at all politely.

"You don't seriously expect us to be ready, do you?" asked one of the recruits, and implied in his tone was an invitation to the corporal to run along and not make a nuisance of himself. This released further torrents of abuse, which persuaded the sixty or so of us who had not yet showered that we had better get out as fast as we could. We therefore began to pour out through the doorway. At this point things became farcical because, far from pleasing the irate corporal, it sent him into a frenzy of anger. Had we not heard him say that everyone must have a shower? Well, he most definitely meant what he said, so what were sixty of us doing sneaking away unwashed? Get back and get on with it, or else. We duly trooped back in but had scarcely begun before a voice shouted: -

"Get on parade."

This was the one thing we cottoned on to quickly. There was safety in numbers and, although we often did little more than damp our hair, we made the corporals wait until everyone had been moistened. Even so there was always a stampede to get back out of the billet once we had dropped our towels. People would emerge with their trousers slipping round their ankles, without their rifles or perhaps without their hats, until eventually we learned that, so long as we did not deliberately go slowly, we could allow ourselves a reasonable time to get ourselves organised.

One morning, the flight sergeant caused a flutter of excitement by announcing a soccer tournament. With the honour of the section at state, and so on and so on, he wanted to put out a team that would take all the other squadrons to the cleaners. All half-decent soccer players were invited to take one pace forward. I hesitated, with Ben's advice that I should never volunteer for anything urging me to stay put. But what could the trap be? Not able to think of one, I stepped forward. Altogether about twenty-five of us volunteered and a corporal came along the line, writing down particulars of the teams we had played for and the position we usually occupied. I was towards the end of the line and the first dozen or so played for Arsenal, Charlton, Spurs, Wolverhampton, Portsmouth, or some other leading club. I was almost too embarrassed to name the county league side I played for and of course, there being no practice match beforehand, I stood no chance of being selected. The evening of the first-round matches arrived, with our 'star-studded' eleven odds-on favourites. We turned out to witness the massacre, and massacre it was. From goalkeeper to left-winger we were, without doubt, the worst eleven ever to disgrace a soccer field. What had gone wrong? There was one good footballer and that was all; the rest had not played for the clubs they mentioned but supported them on the terraces at home matches! The instructors were not amused at having been thus misled and my omission from the side turned out to be no disappointment or disadvantage whatsoever.

This early fiasco was soon forgotten as we faced the hurdle of officer selection. The minimum qualification was three passes at School Certificate which was all right in my case and, indeed, all but one of the twenty-five who put themselves forward easily exceeded this requirement. We had no idea of what qualities they might be looking for beyond leadership at school and, equally, no idea of what we might be letting ourselves in for. My appointment, I remember, was for a quarter past twelve. I made my way to the interview room, imagining myself, en route, in some Walter Mitty role, resplendent in magnificent uniform and bedecked with medals. Instructed to wait until summoned by the interviewing officer, I stood listening outside the hall.

Behind a closed door, my interrogator was speaking to someone on the telephone.

"Yes" he was saying. "I'd love to have lunch with you. About twelve thirty, I should think. We'll have a drink beforehand. Sounds lovely. Oh yes, I know it's twelve fifteen already, but I've only got one more of these tiresome little men to see and I'll soon get rid of him. See you shortly then." He rang off, prepared himself to dismiss me summarily and then called me in.

"Come in, airman, and hurry up about it." Not a bit like his telephone voice. "What's your name again?"

"Morrison, sir."

"Um. What makes you think you are officer material?" And before I could dredge up an answer he went on. "Are you interested in classical music? Do you know anything about it?"

I listened to it, but I was not an expert or a devotee, was all I could honestly tell him.

"Pity. That will be all." He would be early for his luncheon date.

I have to admit that I was disappointed as much by the thoroughly unprofessional way in which I had been interviewed as by the fact that I had obviously been rejected. It would have taken little perception to guess that the only one of our intake who moved beyond the preliminary stage of selection was the only one without the necessary minimum academic qualifications, but he was a music lover. I was depressed by the affair for a little while, not knowing that being turned down had saved me from duties I would have been given on my permanent camp that would have tied me to the camp.

The mood was soon swept away on the tide of ever increasing activity which, whatever else it might be doing, was undoubtedly making me as fit as I ever was, and, oddly enough, as tired as I had ever been. When I had seen my father or my grandfather cropping off to sleep in their chairs at home I had never understood how such a thing could come about and believed that there was no way that I would ever do such a thing. Unthinkable at the age of eighteen. I was very soon to change my mind. During the afternoon, about twice or three times a week, we were given instruction on aircraft recognition. This took place in a sort of lecture theatre, blacked out to allow the showing of slides. We had been rushing about for eight hours prior to the lecture and were just ready for a rest. The man in charge would drone on about various planes, showing slides of each one seen from below, above, head on, inside out and so on. Within minutes heads were nodding as most people enjoyed a welcome nap. The turning on of the lights stirred us into renewed activity and we filed out little the wiser about all those aircraft we were supposed to be recognising.

All went well until our lecturer informed us one day that we would be tested on what we had learned and that anyone failing to gain the pass mark would be in serious trouble. We still could not keep awake. Salvation came in the shape of the airman who worked the projector, as he provided one of our flight with a list of the answers. Thus reassured, we slept contentedly through the last lectures and approached the test brimming with confidence. Our ploy, however, had been discovered, and, at the last minute, the running order was altered - without the projectionist being able to warn us of the change. I was not alone in that I did not even bother to look at the slides being shown on the screen, preferring just to copy down the answers from my crib-sheet. Even I would have realised, had I looked up, that a Hurricane did not have four engines. I scored a paltry three out of twenty but was not required to repeat the test. Apart from a general telling-off about our poor showing, nothing else was done. At least we made a good impression marching back to our quarters.

Marching, in fact, was the backbone of all our training. We didn't walk or stroll or make our way to anywhere; we marched. It wasn't too long before we literally got into the swing of it and we soon learned the little tricks of our instructors. Once we had learnt to keep in straight lines, to swing our arms in unison and to do the various turns, we would respond keenly to the word of command. Knowing that we were straining like greyhounds at the start, our corporal would catch us out:

"Flight, arrrr ..tennnner...shun. By the left, qui -ick." Bodies leaned forward, anticipating the next word of command. Men, over-committed, overbalanced. "Wait for it, wait for it," came the reprimand as the whole line wobbled untidily.

"As you were. By the left qui..ick." This time we were not to be tricked so we laid back on our heels. "March," he snapped, and we were not quite sharp enough.

"Don't hang about like pregnant ducks. Let's see you getting away smartly." We were fair game and we enjoyed the contest.

My own marching made reasonable progress, and yet, while it might be technically sound, it would never entirely be to the liking of the sergeant in charge until I was equipped with proper square-bashing boots. They still hadn't arrived, and the flight sergeant was able to extract a little humour from the situation.

"Some of you lads is of a nervous disposition and I wants you to have as few shocks as possible. So, if one morning you looks out of your window and sees two submarines coming down the path, don't worry. Thems ain't submarines, thems is Morrison's boots." That was one of his better jokes and I didn't really mind, beyond feeling somewhat self-conscious. Then, one morning, a month after we first arrived at the camp, a triumphant announcement.

"I've got some very good news for you lads this morning", the flight sergeant beamed.

A week's extra leave, we wondered. National service has been abolished and we can all go home for good? No.

"Morrison's boots has arrived." A spontaneous cheer went up.

"Well go on then, laddie. Trot up to the stores and fetch them, sharpish."

I hurried to try on the long-awaited boots. They were all right, so I hastily returned to the flight. A warm welcome was waiting.

"They'll need a lot of polishing, laddie and you'll need a lot of polish to cover them. And when I comes to inspect them, why, it'll be just like reviewing the fleet."

The banter ceased after that, but it took me some days to acclimatise to the hardness and the clatter of the studs, and even longer to work up a really good shine on the boots. No matter, I was fully kitted out at last.

I was most uncomfortable in my new square-bashers the following evening. From time to time we used to go down to Hoylake Beach, which was a mile or two away. Before setting out, we changed into our running shorts and singlets, wore our studded boots, and carried our plimsolls. Thus we marched and doubled down to the beach, and so it was that my new footwear got its first long outing. Why we couldn't wear our plimsolls to run to Hoylake was a mystery - but it was not permitted. Once at the beach, we then changed into our plimsolls before going on to the beach to play forty-five-a-side rugby, with the sea wall as one boundary and the water's edge as the other. During the game I came as near to death as I have ever been. The ball came to me in open space and I was pretty sure I could make it to the try line. I had sadly misjudged the distance and my own powers of acceleration. The pitch was about four hundred yards long and I must have been at least fifty yards from my objective, when what seemed like an entire regiment pounced on me. I was pressed face down into the sand as body after body piled on top of me. As my nose and mouth became buried, I felt that my end had come.

Whether the instructor had realised what was happening or whether it was sheer chance, I just do not know, but suddenly everybody was scrambling clear with a real sense of urgency. I was glad that they were, for I doubt if I would have lasted much longer. It was quickly over, however, and the game resumed. If the ball came to me after that I passed it with lightning speed. I had no wish to repeat the experience. The subsequent run back to camp, together with the rest of the day's activities, raised a number of blisters on my feet, so that by the evening I was hobbling about. I was supposed to wear the boots for drilling but, when I tried them on the next morning, I could barely get along in them, so I went back to my best boots for the day and no one seemed to notice. It was not too long before they were fully broken in, but I was never entirely comfortable in them and I virtually abandoned them after leaving West Kirby.

4. SHORT BACK AND SIDES

"Am I hurting you, laddie?" The sergeant asks sarcastically.

"No, Sarge."

"Well I flaming should be. I'm standing on your 'air."

This merry, but stale, little quip comes from page one of the instructor's guide to instant humour. For the first two or three times it's mildly amusing but after a week or so, its predictability makes laughter, even of the forced or subdued variety, an unlikely response. Behind the original question, however, lies the threat or promise of a haircut, and for reasons of appearance, discipline, cleanliness and finance few things were more important.

To look smart, a man must have short hair, preferably no longer than an inch anywhere, but provided that shaggy hair can be concealed beneath a hat then it may be slightly longer in places. The 'lavatory brush 'cut is what should be aimed at. Take off too much, reducing the recruit to a stubbled billiard-ball, and the instructor loses two vulnerable areas of attack; one, discipline, because if you do leave him with that little bit extra under the hat, you can always punish him for long hair if there is nothing else you can get him for; two, unless you leave enough you will lose your commission with the camp barbers to whom you take your recruits at least three times as often as is necessary.

No conscript haircut was memorable, but the first one was so typical of the treatment to come that it was impossible to forget.

It was our second day at Padgate and we were still shambling about in our civilian clothes, being aimlessly chivvied from one place to another, when a moustachioed human loud-hailer screamed, "Haircut". Although this man clearly had more stripes than intelligence, nearly all of us grasped immediately what he was trying to tell us. We were herded towards what appeared to be two small, derelict huts, one of which was the barber's hut and the other an apology for a waiting room. It was raining. There were two hundred and ninety-two of us with room for no more than forty in the empty hut. There were eight of them, eight people that is to cut our hair. You notice that the word barber or hairdresser has been avoided in introducing these eight in the enemy camp, because neither term would be even vaguely applicable to them. Most of them were failed novice sheep shearers who had produced more mutton than fleece and the analogy to sheep was most appropriate, since we went, as it were, like lambs to the slaughter.

The first eight recruits were bundled into the shearing room and were out again so quickly that it appeared as though we had had a temporary reprieve. Then those nearest let out howls of derision and disbelief as they surveyed the damage. The victims seemed to have ears twice the normal size surrounded by a misshapen wire brush. Initially, those not yet processed howled with laughter at their scalped brethren but, as more and more emerged, the mood became one of muted anger as in less than one hour we were all clipped.

Then it was my turn. I have never attributed any Samsonian power to my very average thatch, so I was not particularly apprehensive about a short haircut. The manner of it was, however, one to which only exception could be taken. The room was by this time hair-strewn and steamy. My executioner had a cigarette stub in his mouth, a comb in one hand and electric clippers in the other; there was an ominous absence of scissors. Well into his stride by now, he approached the removal of my hair as though he were ploughing a field - parallel swoops with the clippers, back and forth, with as few sweeps as possible, maybe five or six. He then dipped his hand towards a pot of recycled axle grease, a clot of which he obviously intended to smear on my head. One thing I have always disliked is having any sort of hair cream on my head, preferring to wash the grease out rather than to rub it in.

“I don't want any of that muck on,” I indicated.

"You ain’t got a lot of choice, mate. Either you have it on or you have more hair off."

"Even you couldn't trim any more", I dared.

"Couldn't I?” he threatened, picked up his plough and cut two more furrows. The whole of this delicate operation had taken less than a minute and, tiring of his sport, he bundled me out of the chair.

The bunch outside, sated as they were, even so found something new to marvel at as I emerged, with sympathy outweighing scorn by a considerable margin. The only thing that grieved me was that they had had the gall to charge me a shilling for something I could have sued them for in civilian life. It did not honestly concern me how I looked but for some others in the billet it was a very serious matter indeed. One chap in particular was manifestly proud of his manly crop of wavy golden hair. Even in the first twenty-four hours of our acquaintance, he was frequently to be seen catching sight of himself in the mirror, all the while smoothing his lengthy locks with a fussy hand. He was not spared. In fact, I swear that he was deliberately humiliated. I had thought my hair was short but I had a positive stack compared with him, and when we returned to the billet he went straight to the mirror for one brief glance, threw himself on his bed and cried.

A couple of hours later, we were all crying with laughter, a rare occurrence during the next ten weeks. Relieved to find that we were not going to be run through a sheep dip, most of us washed what was left of our hair. We discovered that rubbing in the shampoo vigorously was very similar to rubbing one's hand along a scrubbing brush, with a fine spray of water flying from the tops of our heads. Then we discovered that the berets, with which we had previously been issued but had not yet worn because we were still in civilian clothes, were far too big. They just flopped down loosely until their descent was blocked by our ears. I could barely see out from under mine and it never did fit properly again. Looking round as others tried on their now ill-fitting headgear, we indulged in a much-needed laugh. This time the tears from our blonde companion were of enjoyment.

After that first Monday haircut, we only stayed another two days at Padgate before transferring to West Kirby where, on the Thursday morning, we were soon guided to the hairdressing section. It was still much too early for us to work out what exactly was going on, but we were, nevertheless, astonished to find that, in both senses of the word, we were to be clipped again. A perfectly good reason was given. The Easter grant began that very day with everybody leaving camp at noon. They wanted us to be smart, a credit to our station, and that meant above all else we must have tidy hair. Only short hair was tidy hair so no doubt we would agree that, after three whole days, we needed a haircut. To say that we marched to our second fleecing would be less than the truth, because we were raw novices, an absolute shower, as our flight sergeant never tired of reminding us. We shambled along, half-wondering if a joke were being played on us, all ninety-eight of us far too green to know that everything was in deadly earnest.

Not so many barbers this time and all of us in and out even more quickly than at Padgate. Another shilling out of our pockets. No time to worry about that, as we had to tear round in order to be ready to leave camp at mid-day. Because we had only been at the camp for twenty-four hours, it had not been possible to organise any special transport for us. We marched down to West Kirby station and were left to our own devices. Getting to Norwich by train from this remote place, via Liverpool, was a long, tedious business and it was well into the early hours of Friday morning before I finally arrived home. Not in the least bit tired but ravenously hungry for proper food again, the more so since the scent of gently frying bacon tickled my nostrils on entering, I was confronted by my sister. She was as anxious to see me in my uniform as I was for her not to. Now remember, I had undergone two mowings in four days, so that the slightest movement of my head caused my hat to swivel and droop. Able only to see the toes of my shoes as I went into the sitting-room, I hastily removed my beret. My sister burst into hysterical laughter; my Mother, sensing my discomfiture, assured me that it looked very smart, and my Grandfather muttered: -

"Blast if that ent a rummun!"

The vote had gone against me, two to one, and within the warm company of my own family I could definitely see the funny side of things.

"Whatever have they done to your hair;" my sister persisted. "Removed it", I replied coolly.

And another peal of her laughter persuaded me to join in. It really was rather comical, but it certainly was not smart. Then another thought occurred to me. We had been forbidden to wear civilian clothes on our leave but had no intention of heeding the warning. Trouble was that, even out of uniform, our haircuts betrayed us as recruits, like prison uniforms patterned with arrows, and come to think of it, for the next eighteen months we were virtual prisoners.

This sombre realisation was rammed home by my sister's next question.

"When do you go back?"

It was ever to be thus. As soon as I got home, they wanted to know when I was going back, whereas I wanted to forget about it. What they actually meant (I think) was that they hoped I would be staying a long time but my first, erroneous impression was that they would be relieved when I returned to camp.

And return I did, to start the serious business of square-bashing on the Tuesday after Easter. Since, at some time or other, all the non-commissioned officers we confronted warned us of their extremely dubious parentage and its likely dire consequences for us, we were not in the least worried or surprised when our own allotted corporal threatened us with similar retribution. What did surprise us were his opening instructions.

"All you lot 'ave been away on yer 'olidays and I don't suppose one of you ever thought about 'avin yer 'air cut. Well, we'll soon put that right by going down there now."

He was absolutely right, of course, not one of us had given it a thought. So, off we went again for yet another trim, with the time taken over the job even shorter than before. That was the Tuesday and we heard nothing more about haircuts right up until the Friday of that same week. It must have slipped their minds, because the matter was left until after lunch when the corporal used a different approach: -

"Expect all you lads could do with a ten-minute break, so we'll nip down to the barbers to tidy up your hair for the weekend." And with that, off we went again.

The 'barbers' at West Kirby were civilians but not very civil, you understand, and by this time we had worked out the reason for our regular visits. Remember that we paid one shilling each and there were ninety-eight of us in the flight. Near enough five pounds in their pockets every time we were trimmed. Even allowing for the fact that we had been off the camp for four days, this was our third haircut in eight days, and our fourth in twelve days, counting the one at Padgate. The instructors, of course, worked on a commission basis with the civilian barbers, so the more often they took us, the more money for them both. Supposing the instructors took only twenty per cent, it was enough to keep them comfortably in beer and cigarettes. The mystery was solved, and we settled into a pattern of about two haircuts a week for the next two months, it being useless to protest that we did not need one.

Some recruits had more trouble than they deserved over their hair, through no fault of their own. We had one of these unfortunate men in our flight. He was swarthy and had an extremely dark growth of hair on his chin and face, so that immediately after he had given himself a good shave he still looked unshaven. He was not in the least bit an offensive type, rather quiet and reserved actually, but he was picked out to be made an example of. It all began just a couple of days after we arrived at West Kirby, when, a couple of hours after having given a pint of blood, he collapsed on parade. His fault, naturally, and no excuse to be found for such feeble behaviour. It would be no exaggeration to say that he was victimised for the rest of his basic training, but he took it all stoically until the Whitsun grant. This time we had been able to book on coaches provided by the RAF for most destinations. His coach left first but he was not on it.

About twenty minutes before we were due to leave, the instructors inspected our appearance. The swarthy chap was told he had not shaved and was sent off to shave before he could go, while we waited. He returned, red-faced and flustered, to be met with another of the regulation little quips.

"Did you shave then, laddie?"

“Yes, corporal."

"Well, I suggest you stand closer to the razor next time. Go and try again."

This went on three times, while meantime many of us had gone to our coaches, and he eventually was made to miss his coach. But it did not end there. His father had died and he had requested a compassionate posting to a base close to his home, so that he could help out his mother. They sent him to Germany for the rest of his national service!

5. TARGET PRACTICE

I have never been much of a one for shooting at things, living or dead. Just occasionally, when harvesting at Church Farm in Norfolk, my uncle would prevail upon me to go round the fields with his gun. I was always mightily relieved on the rare occasions when I did fire to find that I had missed. What finally persuaded me to stop going out with a gun at all was a terrible experience. I had walked up to a spinney to scare off some pigeons. It was beginning to get dark and I fired up into the treetops as a pigeon flew in to land. Something crashed heavily to the ground and as I went to recover it I found to my dismay that I had shot an owl. That was a long time ago and I have still not completely forgiven myself, but at least I haven't shot at anything since.

Weapon training and rifle shooting, therefore, held little interest for me and, with my background of inhibitions, it was only to be expected that I would not be very good in these areas of training. I could never imagine myself sticking a bayonet into a fellow human being although I suppose, if it came down to a question of life or death, I would react instinctively to save my own skin. There was, nevertheless, something unreal about bayonet practice. Even the instructors, as they demonstrated the "In, out, on guard" technique of boring an enemy to death, lacked conviction. Unlike the yelling maniacs seen on the cinema screen from time to time, apparently revelling in every life-sapping thrust. However, we had to go through the motions of fixing bayonets, nine inches of round, cold steel, charging at a dummy and stabbing it by numbers. The bayonet, like the overcoat, was another one of those sacred objects more valuable apparently than the recruit himself. The flights about to pass out from the camp always seemed to be one or two short and it became the recognized practice to steal them from the junior entries to avoid any deficiency in their equipment when they checked out of the camp for good. It was a continuing process; as the junior entry itself became senior, then it had to make good its loss from the next intake, and so on. The only practical use bayonets were ever put to was in a rather sadistic form of punishment devised by the instructors. The ground between our huts was solid clay and therefore difficult to be made looking presentable. Defaulters were given the task of digging the ground with their nine-inch bayonets, held in their bare hands. The temptation was to clip the bayonet into the rifle to give much needed extra leverage, but this was forbidden and led to even more dire punishment. After a couple of hours digging in this fashion hands became blistered and extremely sore, with progress painfully slow. Sometimes, to make the punishment more interesting, the corporal would have the freshly dug clay marched over so that it then needed turning over again. Bayonets took on a very special meaning for a few, unlucky recruits, who, as a result, may have changed their minds about ever bringing themselves to use them in combat with another man.

I have always tried to see the lighter side of a situation and tried to extract from it whatever humour it contained. Weapon training and its allied crafts provided one or two amusing episodes. We were being trained in the art of camouflage, with our instructors almost as much in the dark as we were, thus it was one of the few things not taken seriously. There we were, in acres of space, completely without cover, save for one very small clump of bushes some fifty yards away in the centre of the location.

"Right lads," we were urged, "on the word of command I want you all to spread out and make yourselves invisible." That was all very well but there were several dozen of us with very little prospect of concealing ourselves anywhere, especially after the next piece of advice.

"Now you see that clump of bushes over there? Yes, well that's the obvious place to hide, isn't it? And where will the enemy look for you first? – in the most obvious place. So it's no use you all rushing over there, is it? You've got to be cleverer than that and find a more unlikely hiding place." Sound advice, but where to go on a stretch of flat, barren land. Where did the corporal suggest?

"Suggest? You wouldn't have me to wet nurse you in a crisis, would you? You'd have to use your own initiative." He didn't know the answer to his own problem. Someone asked if we would be carrying spades with us and whether a few swiftly dug holes might do the trick. He did not think that was a very practical suggestion, since the enemy was almost upon us and we had only moments to become invisible. Tired of this fruitless exchange of ideas, the corporal gave the word of command: -

"Move!"

Still grappling with the problem, I stayed put while the rest rushed over the open space and, one by one, dropped to the ground where, from my standpoint, they resembled so many human molehills. For the moment I had forgotten that I was supposed to be one of them. In that endearing manner developed through years of incomparable experience, the instructor strutted up to me and, with his face at least four inches from mine, yelled: -

"Morrison, I thought I flaming told you to spread out!"

Knowing my man, I stretched my arms wide in the manner of a scarecrow.

"Move!" he screamed, and I trotted over to the bush to make myself the only member of the squad out of sight.

So much for camouflage. What about patrols in enemy territory? Here was a thing in which every self-respecting airman needed guidance, particularly in peacetime. Wearing our denims, we set out on a simulated patrol. We must trust our instructor implicitly and obey his every command instantly, however stupid or unreasonable it might seem. We were used to that, anyway. Failure to respond might jeopardise the whole group. Making our way through a muddy patch of ground, we were suddenly given the order: -

"Down!"

All but one of us flung ourselves to the ground. To the repeated command "Down," the airman still upright protested: -

"You don't think I'm going to lay down in that mess, do you?"

This was one of those moments when action and not words was far more effective. In a flash the corporal was on his feet and had tripped the airman's legs from under him. He crashed unceremoniously into the mud, the lesson learned. All this blind obedience to tiresome orders had, at a stroke fallen into place. So had the protesting recruit.

However much I disliked them, guns could not be avoided. We made regular visits to the rifle range, where they rattled on about two pressures on the trigger, or was it two triggers on the pressure? I'm not sure and I was not that interested. From time to time we fired a few rounds into a small target; I counted myself lucky to hit the protecting wall, let alone the miniscule target. As we progressed we were introduced to Sten guns. These we had to dismantle and reassemble each time before using. They were like a simplified bicycle pump and were as dangerous to the user as to the enemy they were aimed at. There was a minute finger guard where the left hand gripped the shortish barrel and failure to locate this stop could cause the top of the left little finger to be projected along with the first round. There must be scores of people around with the top joint of this finger missing for that very reason. One or two of the instructors could hit something with one of these guns but few recruits, and certainly not me, were given the chance to fire them. Those that did got nowhere near the target and, since the barrel of the Sten gun was so short compared with the rifles we used, it only needed the gun to be turned slightly sideways to become an instant threat to half the squadron. I was always very pleased and relieved when a Sten gun session came to an end.

All this high-powered training culminated in a series of tests which, it goes without saying, it was absolutely imperative for us to pass. Assault course, bayonet practice and camouflage were just a few of the tests we had to go through. As each individual recruit completed a given test, he reported to his assessor for a grade. This grade took the form of a colour. So, for bayonet work, you might be told your classification was red; for another blue or maybe yellow or green. As we worked our way through each test, we compared notes with others: -

"How are you getting on so far?"

"I've got two greens, a red and a purple."

"I can beat that with three blues and a pink."

We had to remember these colours in our heads and we had absolutely no idea which colours took precedence. When all the tests were over, I think there were seven or eight of them, the roll was then called and each recruit answered to his name with the colours he had been given.

"Anderson."

"Two reds, two browns, a yellow, pink and a blue."

"Hughes?"

"Three reds, three blues and a green." Gasps of admiration.

Then, the bombshell.

"Nelson."

"Heliotrope, cyan, two mustards, two magentas and puce!"

Roars of laughter. His assessing corporal had seen the funny side of it and that was the answer. The colours were absolutely meaningless, but the pretence had been marvellously kept going until the end. It was over and it had turned out to be good fun at the death.

Then there was the matter of the final assessment on the rifle range - there could be no fooling about there. The really outstanding shots could also qualify for a marksman's badge which brought them a few extra shillings a week in their wages. I was not altogether confident of an increase in my criminally small wage of twenty-eight shillings a week. In small batches, we were called forward to take the test. When it came to my turn, I found myself allocated to the number three position. We were given ten rather lethal looking bullets and, under necessarily strict supervision, were ordered to our places.

"In your own time, ten rounds, fire," came the command. "And hurry up about it."

I inserted a bullet, aimed in the general direction of the number three target, and jerked the trigger into action. Opening my eyes, I could not see exactly where the shot landed but there was a definite dent in the bullseye. First one ever. Competition was bringing out the Wyatt Earp in me. Eagerly I slotted the second round into the hole. Let me get at that target. Bang! Another piece ripped out of the bullseye. There was no stopping me now. I could not reload fast enough. Four, five, six – that bullseye was disintegrating. I had to press on while the spell lasted. Or did I? Should I not calm down a little from this frenzy of excitement? Didn't want to blow my marksman's badge. No. Steady down. Seven, bang in the middle; eight, right next to it; nine, another perfect shot. One to go and I would be in the money. I closed my eyes for the last time and there it was – a perfect score.

Most people had finished, and I waited impatiently while the remaining few discharged their last rounds. Then the order to down rifles and collect targets. I must have been having my Mitty dream again but, as I closed in on the number three target, there could be no mistake about it. The centre of the target was completely blasted away, leaving just a jagged hole. Proudly I joined the queue to have my target scrutinised. Still not believing my eyes I showed no one my target, instead I waited for the corporal to confirm my perfect marksmanship. He took my card and after close inspection called out: -

"Ten in the bull."

At the same time as he said this a voice somewhere behind me was complaining; -

"'Ere corporal. There ain't nuffing on my target."

My own corporal had arrived by this time.

"What's this then, Morrison? A maximum score. Don't believe it. You've never had one on the target before. What you been up to?"

My hopes of a marksman's badge were diminishing by the second, even though the mystery remained unsolved for the time being. The bloke with 'nuffing' on his target would not go away. In fact, his instructor was complaining that this potential sharpshooter could not possibly have scored a zero.

Meanwhile the scrutineer was re-examining my target. Yes, there was definitely a solid grouping of ten in the bullseye but what was that faintest of nicks in the top left-hand corner? Well off the actual circle of the target but on the extreme edge of the square of card was an unmistakable mark. A careful recount showed that there were not ten but eleven shots on my card. Then the crushing blow.

"What target were you aiming at then?" the complaining airman was asked.

"Number three target, of course," was the devastating reply.

"And you, Morrison?"

“Number three target,” disconsolately.

“That’s it then, isn’t it? You were both firing at the same target.”

At least I had been using the right one but there were no prizes for that. It was decided that my neighbour who should have been shooting at number four target was a marksman, with his maximum score. And me? Well, I hadn’t any cause for complaint, for I was well aware that the ten bullseyes were not mine. I am not sure what would have happened if the mistake had gone undiscovered. Would I have been included in the shooting teams? And what about the extra money, under false pretences? Would have taken some justifying. Much as I might like to dream, there was one certain thing for me - bullseyes were out, but bull nights were unavoidably in.

6. BRUSHES WITH AUTHORITY

The one man to avoid at all costs on a camp like West Kirby was the Station Warrant Officer, for such men were sculpted rather than conceived. Men of steel and granite. Pompous, self-important men, mean and shrewd, more formidable than their army equivalents because, relatively speaking, they were more intelligent. The cutting edge, the final polish of a camp, that was down to - and a reflection upon - the SWO. The only two I ever encountered were also of miniscule stature, and, as so often the case with such little men, they compensated for their small frames with a superabundance of bombast. The mixture of small and SWO was explosive. Believing themselves omnipotent, they attempted to render the raw recruit ragged by exploding at him. Shout meaningless obscenities at him until he tries to mumble an incoherent excuse or apology, whereupon you slap him in the guardroom for insolence; or turn him into a speechless statue, and once again you can whisk him away for insolence, this time of the dumb variety. This method of attack meant that their victims were usually some scared, inoffensive unfortunates, who were never going to be any real trouble, but of whom it was easy to make a severe example.

In the later stages of our training the SWO took more than a passing interest. He watched the way our drill was progressing and recruited small groups to go and show the flag at local Sunday parades. Because I was tall I had the misfortune to be selected for one of these, along with seventeen others. We had to put in some extra drill and were joined, late in the day, by another group of eighteen who had been hastily formed to meet a last-minute request for the same Sunday as us. We went off to some local town for the church parade, where the mayor happened to be an ex-RAF officer. He came to speak with us afterwards, thanked us and was clearly delighted that we had not let the service down. He thought, in fact, that we had done well. Feeling quite pleased with ourselves, we wondered how the other group had fared. Evidently they had been a disaster and their mayor had let it be known that he was most disappointed with their efforts. The SWO took a very dim view and, addressing the two groups as one, almost blew a fuse in telling us all off. Guilt by association, I suppose.

About a week later, he was back again with his pace-stick, to give us instructions for our passing-out parade. In particular he wanted to introduce us to the manoeuvre of advancing in review order. The whole squadron groups at the back of the parade ground and receives only the command to advance, completing the rest of the drill without further verbal orders. The SWO explained that we would march forward seventeen paces, which we would count to ourselves, before halting, by ourselves. As a right-marker I was in a rather obvious position, as the SWO gave us our first run through:

"Parade will advance in review order. Dressing from the right…By the right, quick march."

"One, two, three…" I whispered to myself. "Fourteen, fifteen, sixteen, seventeen, eighteen, nineteen…' before I realised what I had done, and I was the only one of nearly three hundred who made a mistake. We practised it a number of times subsequently and there were always several who got it wrong. Not on this occasion, though.

Shouting from somewhere just below the tongue of his left boot, the SWO screamed:

"Get off my square."

Taking him at his word, I began to march off the parade ground towards my billet.

"Where the Halifax do you think you're going?" he bellowed with even greater menace.

What was I to do in this classic situation? I dared not answer and yet was afraid not to. Before I could make the wrong choice, the SWO told me to get back into line and to pull myself together. I never made even a semblance of a mistake from that moment.

A few days later I encountered him again. I had written a letter during the evening, but, before posting it, I slipped into the washing block behind our billet, having first put the letter into my pocket. I then hurried up to the post box in the fading light. On the way back, I was suddenly hailed by a voice I instantly recognised and judged to be at least a hundred yards behind me.

"Airman," it commanded, "come here."

A month earlier I would have turned round guiltily and been trapped into betraying myself. Without batting an eyelid, I kept on walking, telling myself that the SWO might be summoning someone else. Who was I kidding?

The order was repeated in a far more angry voice: -

"Air-man!"

Committed now, I carried on unheeding, feeling that the SWO would not lower his dignity by chasing after me. No, he expected me to crumble. By this time I had doubled the distance between us as I hurriedly worked out my next move. It would be foolish to turn off by my billet, so I carried on some way past it before eventually turning left. As soon as I was shielded by a building, I broke into a frenzied run which, after another left turn, brought me to the rear of my hut. Taking off my beret and composing myself before entering, I made my way quietly to my bed, three spaces from the end, as though just returning from the washing block. Hastily removing my battledress and footwear, I sat down on my bed and began polishing my boots vigorously.

A few moments later the top door was flung open with the usual violence. The corporal wanted to know if any of us had just walked down from the direction of the guard room. I do not think anybody had noticed me because we all vouched for each other in the cause of collective security. The dim figure of the SWO was visible in the background but he seemed quite satisfied by our assurances. After the door had closed it was obvious from the confusion that no one knew what the fuss was about and it seemed safer all round that the secret should remain mine alone.

I never did find out why the SWO at West Kirby was yelling at me but, since I was not aware of having broken any rule, I could only assume that he was about to order me to volunteer for something. I did, however, know exactly what the SWO at Cranwell was pursuing me for. He was a small, smart, stern man, who spoke few words but chose them most carefully. When I first began my daily trek from flying wing to the headquarters building, I would always say good morning as I passed his room by the back entrance. He never once responded, so after a while, I gave up trying. I was certainly not trying to ingratiate myself; rather, I thought it might be considered deliberately discourteous of me to ignore him. The pattern that eventually became established was very much to my advantage because, had I got into the habit of chatting to him every morning, he would have noticed when I wasn't there. I still had to be careful, so I used to vary the time of my arrival when I knew he either would or would not be there, according to what was necessary to cover my tracks. It worked for a good deal longer than I had expected.

One morning in early summer, as I was emerging from my flying wing office at the far end of the passage, a voice from the other end called to me through the open doorway.

"Is that you, Morrison?" It was the flight-sergeant in charge of administration for the section, who had a sort of half-claim on me.

"Yes. What can I do for you?"

"Come in here a minute and I'll tell you."

There were so many things that I could think of that he might want me for that I decided to let him do all the talking, which he probably would have done anyway.

"Got any special plans for the week-end, have you?"

"No, nothing special, flight-sergeant."

"You going to be here on Saturday morning?"

"Well, of course I am. Why do you ask?"

"Don't often see you down this way on a Saturday."

"No, well you wouldn't. I mostly spend Saturday morning up at headquarters."

"Is that a fact? Well, make sure that you are there this Saturday at about ten-thirty."

"Why do you say that?" I enquired nervously.

"Never mind why, just be there."

He really had no reason to give me the chance that he did because there had been nothing better than an armed neutrality between us. It was very fair of him in the circumstances, but he would have his pound of flesh as well.

"When were you last on security patrol, laddie?"

"Ooh…aahh…quite recently I think."

"I don't, because I've checked through orders for the last six months and your name doesn't appear once. Wonder why that is?"

"Can't think of a reason," I lied, knowing full well that my card had been withdrawn from the roster so that I could safely absent myself from camp during the college holidays. I had not done a guard since the previous October.

"Better read station routine orders thoroughly for the next few weeks," He advised." Sometimes people get put on guard four or five times in close succession."

That Friday night in the middle of June was the first time that year I had not been at home for an early weekend. There was a good deal of lively, and well-deserved, leg pulling. Had I mistaken the day or was I not feeling too well? Did I not realise it was Friday and that they had let my bed on a long lease? For the moment, I gave them no explanation for my presence. The corporal in charge of our room weighed in with his own comments, as indeed he was entitled to. He could so easily have reported my regular absences, since they did in some ways compromise him. He had kept quiet though, as everybody else had and, as I lay awake after lights out, I pondered just how lucky I had been. I also resolved to stick rigidly to the rules for my remaining three months because any serious offence might possibly delay my release beyond the start of the university term. All sorts of horrible ideas passed through my head, the worst being the idea of having to serve the extra six months after all. I dropped into a fitful sleep like a man who had just cheated the gallows.

It was strange to wake up on camp on a Saturday morning, but I resigned myself to having to get used to it until the end of September. Breakfast was no better on a Saturday than on any other day, but I needed something before setting out on my later than usual hitch-hike. The flight lieutenant was astonished to see me at flying wing, to the extent that he asked me if everything was all right. Reassured, he went off for his weekend, whereupon the flight sergeant bid me a cheery good morning, with his moustache more stiffly to attention than usual, I thought, and with a perfectly wicked gleam in his eye.

Much earlier than usual, I made my way to the headquarters building, busying myself with the charts in the plans section. The arrival of the mobile canteen just before ten gave me the chance to supplement my disappointing breakfast, until, bang on the stroke of ten-thirty the end door opened and in walked the SWO, accompanied by the flying wing flight sergeant. For once he spoke.

"Good morning," was his civil greeting. "Just come to see what you get up to in here."

"Good morning, Sir. Perhaps you'd like to have a look at some of my charts. They are for the Air Commodore's benefit and are the same as those I have at flying wing for the CFI." I enthused, somewhat obsequiously.

"Very interesting. Keep up the good work." There was more than a tinge of disappointment in his voice, as he made to leave.

"I appreciate your coming, sir." I was crawling now.

"Good day to you laddie." And turning to the flight sergeant,

"That's all very much in order flight. Seems as though I was misinformed, but we'll keep an eye from now on."

The flight sergeant murmured quietly to me as he followed the SWO out:

"Well done lad. Always pays to follow good advice, don't you think?"

I had certainly altered my opinion about that man, just as I was more convinced than ever that my officer had played his part in keeping the bulldogs off me, though he would certainly have denied it.

7. ON GUARD

Guarding a military camp in times of war is a serious business. Failure to do the job properly could lead to the severest punishment and rightly so. Guarding West Kirby in peacetime against unauthorised intruders, when everyone was anxious to get out of the camp and not into it, we regarded as an unnecessary exercise, and rightly so. During their basic training, all recruits were required to do a guard duty although they were very ill-equipped to do so if judged by the example at West Kirby. Ill-equipped because, after only a few weeks' service, they had little idea of how to proceed, and ill-equipped because they were given virtually nothing with which to defend themselves. As with so many things, the chief purpose of the exercise seemed to be to threaten what the consequences might be for a guard improperly executed.

There had been a dance on the camp for which coach loads of young Liverpudlian lasses had been imported. My guard duty began just as the last painful tunes were being hammered out. Although there was no photo-finish in those days the band would not have needed one, for they never finished that close together. The last outlying couples were being rounded up as I made my way to my post, accompanied by the guard sergeant. Bristling with sophisticated equipment, I was shown to a dilapidated sentry box, situated on the bank of a narrow stream. Over this stream was a wooden bridge, one plank wide, which led to married quarters. No one must enter the camp over the bridge without showing the correct pass. To stop any potential intruder, I was armed with an extremely weak torch, a clip-board to which was attached a crumpled sheet of instructions, and the sawn-off leg of a wooden chair some eighteen inches long and two inches in diameter. If anyone did come across during the night, it was likely to be an officer, but I was not told if I should physically obstruct a commissioned officer who tried to force his way in. The sergeant departed with a final warning about not falling asleep.

It did not rain but there was a thick covering of cloud, making the night especially dark. To begin with, I sat inside the box, listening to the noises of the camp finally putting itself to bed, before an intense quiet established itself. Sitting down was not a good idea, my nodding head advised me, so I tried standing up. That was better, even if I leaned against the side, because I could not get comfortable enough to fall asleep, fall being the operative word. I had been in this position for some twenty minutes when a noise from behind the box tightened my every muscle. It was on my side of the stream, moving noisily in my direction. My first instinct was to remain absolutely motionless and allow my adversary to go past and present his back to me before I announced my presence. No, that was no good since it was odds-on that someone inside the camp knew his way around sufficiently well to be aware that the sentry box was manned. In which case he would spring on me suddenly and I would be trapped inside, probably with a knife in my giblets. The element of surprise would be mine if I attacked first - but then it occurred to me that it might be the sergeant, checking to see if I had fallen asleep. In the end I compromised by standing half in and half out of the sentry box, slightly turned towards the stream as that was the side where the noise was. I waited for him to make his move.

My eyes had become accustomed to the darkness, so that I could see vague outlines, and in any case, I did not wish to betray my position by shining the torch. The noise was now within a yard or two of coming into view, then, with a shuffle and a snuffle it came into sight. A hedgehog, a pretty large hedgehog mind you. With relief and amusement I watched him trundle down the gradually sloping bank in search of water. As he drank noisily I noticed that I was shaking. Unkindly, I planned to give him a scare to match the one he had given me. Eventually he came scrambling up the bank, still unaware of my presence. As he drew level, I barked at him loudly, causing him to grunt in surprise and scurry away.

It seemed quieter than ever after the hedgehog had gone but it had so stirred me up that there was now no danger of my dropping off to sleep. No chance of that anyway, with the sound of footsteps coming along the path from married quarters. I had undoubtedly been scared before by the hedgehog, but I felt fully in control now. I moved to my end of the bridge to bar the way. I had been told to expect an officer and the advice had been sound. As he stepped on to the far end of the bridge I challenged him: -

“Halt: Who's there?"

“It's all right, airman. I'm squadron leader Barnes. I'm on my way up to the guard room."

“May I see your pass please, sir?"

He searched briefly through his pockets.

"I don't seem to have it but you can let me pass. I'm the guard commander."

"I'm sorry, sir, but I'm not allowed to let you in unless you show the correct pass."

"Do you realise who I am? It'll go badly for you if you persist in this nonsense."

"I was told that I would be court-martialled if I allowed anyone through without a pass."

"Well I'll see to it that you are charged if you continue to hold me up. I'm late already."

He was apparently very angry by now but that somehow strengthened my resolve. I did not really see how I could be punished for following orders; whereas there seemed to be very real danger in allowing him to browbeat me into agreeing. I realised that I was actually enjoying myself but there remained this one doubt about what would happen to me if I was obliged to oppose the squadron-leader physically because the penalties for laying a hand on a commissioned officer were severe. He tried once more.

"If you think that I am going to walk all the way back to my house for my pass when I have crossed this bridge hundreds of times without it, you are mistaken."

"I can't allow you by, sir, without your pass."

"I'll have your name and number right now, airman, and I shall report you as soon as I get to the guardroom."

"I am only doing what I was told to do, sir."

He accepted the situation and stormed off back to his house. Just a few minutes later he returned, thrust the correct pass at me and disappeared into the darkness in a black mood.

For the rest of my duty at the bridge, I could think of little else but what awaited me on my return to the guardroom. It was just after four in the morning when I got back, to find the room empty. I lay down on the floor and was asleep almost at once. I was so tired that, even on such an uncomfortable 'bed', nothing disturbed me for six hours. I woke up with water running over my head and neck. The sergeant had shouted at me to wake up, but it had had no effect, so he poured a jug of cold water over me. He told me that I had greatly upset the squadron leader, that he did not know what would happen to me, but he would do the best he could to ease things for me.

After he had gone out, I heard two service policeman saying that they would like to get their hands on that Morrison bloke and they would not like to be in his shoes when the punishment was dished out. I was seized with panic for I had not realised that I could be in such dire trouble. With the door ajar I heard other references to my name which only further alarmed me. At length, the sergeant came back with the verdict: -

“You're a lucky lad, do you know that?" he breezed.

“How lucky?" I stammered.

"Lucky you stuck to your guns and didn't let the squadron leader over the bridge. He was angry about leaving his pass at home rather than with you. If you had let him over you would have been for the high jump. As it is, he commended me for instilling into you recruits the need to stick to the rules. Well done laddie."

So the sergeant was pleased, the squadron leader was not, after all, dis-pleased, and I was in the clear.

What of the threats I had heard being uttered against me by the service policeman? I asked the sergeant why they should have been so sure that I was going to get it in the neck. For a moment he was puzzled before he was able to put my mind at rest. There was another recruit with the same surname as mine, but with the initial S, who kept running away from the camp. Although he had been in the Air Force for eight months, he had only completed three weeks of basic training. Given the slightest chance, he was over the wall and away. They had just recaptured him for the umpteenth time and brought him back under guard. I felt sorry for him in a way and I wondered how long they would confine him before finally letting him go. At his current rate of progress, he would be two years finishing his square bashing.

At Cranwell, the guard duty was called security patrol, which operated from one of the condemned huts on west camp, separate from the main guardroom. The hut, especially the toilet and wash-basin, was squalid in the extreme because, with a different group of people manning it each night, it was never properly cleaned. It smelt revolting and I counted myself extremely fortunate that I only did one security patrol in my first year. What a night it was! It rained and blew incessantly. I was due out with another airman at midnight, but it was so bad that we thought we might be told to stay in the hut. Our hopes were even higher when the first pair came back saturated and exhausted, but they were soon dashed. The show must go on and we were next on stage.

We had a huge area to cover with various checkpoints listed, at any of which the guard commander might turn up at the time stated to check that we were carrying out our duties correctly. We both had our groundsheets with us which helped to keep our shoulders and backs dry, together with the usual feeble torch, checklist and stick. We set off at twelve for the first location on our list. Nobody turned up except us, soaking wet and bedraggled. We gambled that no officer would be fool enough to turn out in such foul weather and made our way to the nearest barrack block. Once there, we quietly sought out the drying room, which was comfortably warm, and we sat down to chat away the time until we were due to return to the guard hut. Inevitably, we both went to sleep in such cosy surroundings. Neither of us woke up in time and when I finally stirred and asked my partner the time, we were half an hour overdue.

We had slept for about two hours, during which time we had dried out and, since we were only a stone's throw from the guard hut, we felt that we could not go back in such an obviously dry state. We therefore struck out in the opposite direction to the guard hut to spend ten minutes getting ourselves thoroughly gunged up and soaked. We then staggered into the hut in a distressed and dishevelled state to make our apologies to the guard NCO. We told how the elements had slowed our progress and how we had feared to cut corners, lest we should miss the guard-commander at a checkpoint. Being conscientious to a fault had made us late but we had thought that better than skimping our duty. Did not the NCO think that was the wisest thing? Well, yes he did, and he was sorry we had got so wet in the process, we need not worry about returning late - he quite understood. Nothing more was said about the matter and I don’t suppose any report was made either about the guard commander not turning up at any of the checkpoints throughout the night. It was like saluting in corridors, it depended upon how you interpreted the rules and what rank you held.

8. STRAIGHT ANSWERS

When I arrived home for the Whitsun Grant, the family made no comment about my hairstyle, though I fancy my father was tempted to make war-whooping chants as would a Red Indian on the warpath. Naturally, their opening question was to ask when I went back, but most of all they wondered how much weight I had put on during the six weeks that I had been away at West Kirby. I have always been lean of build and able to pack away food without any noticeable sign of expansion. From a small boy, my parents had marvelled at the way I would be ravenously hungry after a huge meal, to be seen half an hour later gnawing away at a crust of bread I had filched from the larder. The basic food that we were served on camp was high in starch content though never sufficient to make you feel that you had overeaten and I had taken the slightly chubbier look around my cheeks to be due to a lack of hair, revealing in greater detail the contour of my face. I was sure that my weight had not increased significantly, only to be proved wrong when I stepped on the scales. I was a whole stone heavier than my normal weight and yet, indisputably, fitter than ever before. So, whatever else it was doing to me, square bashing was keeping me in splendid health.

On that Friday evening, one of the prospective candidates for the South Norfolk parliamentary constituency was addressing a meeting in the village, which I was anxious to attend to put to him a most pertinent question. Well, I thought it was anyway. After a laboriously dull introduction by the chairman, the candidate said his lengthy, and even duller, party piece before throwing the meeting open to questions. Betrayed by my haircut, though not in uniform, I caught the chairman's eye at the fifth attempt.

“Yes, young man, what is your question?"

“Do you not think that, if a man is old enough to serve his country at the age of eighteen, possibly to be sent to and killed in Korea, then he should be entitled to vote at parliamentary elections?" Murmurs of approval gave me hopes of a rousing, positive answer.

With a look of resigned benevolence the candidate replies: -

"That is a good question, a very good question indeed, from a young man who is obviously, at this very moment, serving his country most loyally. Only the other day I was talking to a national serviceman in my village whose mother takes in washing and is also renowned for the delicious home preserve she makes. Her lemon curd is delectable and she has some home-made pickle recipes that are out of this world. And I said to this young fellow, it’s people like you and your mother who make this old country of ours worth fighting for. If we can raise the standard of living, as indeed our leader pledged to do at the Blackpool conference, build more houses and put a few more hops in the beer then all the sacrifices we have made in the past will seem worthwhile. Yes, a good question. Next."

"But what is the answer to my question? Will your party...."

The chairman intervened: -

"You've had your question and now kindly sit down and give others a chance."

Another first experience had been chalked up to me- never expect a politician to give a direct answer to a direct question.

Returning from the grant was a good deal easier than at Easter, with the prospect of a full week's leave only three weeks away. We were one of the more senior groups on the camp by this time. We were used to the system and the raw edges of our inexperience were not so obvious. When you are under intense and unaccustomed pressure, it is odd how a few weeks, which in reality are as nothing, can assume such importance. We were, however, still no match for our instructors. With the exception of those required as billet orderlies, two per hut, the recruits had a day off. They were at liberty to leave the camp for once. Informing us of this, our tender-hearted corporal asked for sympathy to be shown towards the two unfortunate airmen who would have to stay behind to mind the billet. Wouldn't it be a good idea to have a whip round for them to help soften the blow? A shilling each plus one from him would net twenty-four shillings, twelve shillings for each of the two. We willingly chipped in and guess who had the money?

We must have been rich pickings to those hardened campaigners but I, for one, did not realise at the time. The most blatant way in which I was exploited was, without doubt, during our week of squadron fatigues. Fatigues are usually considered a punishment, and indeed they could be. They frequently took the form of some completely useless task, such as running round the parade ground for half an hour with a heavy wooden kit-box on your back; or whitewashing the outer edge of a pile of coke, which could only be achieved by sloshing the stuff on in a sort of spraying movement - and then, just as you had finished going round the pile, a figure would emerge to shovel away a quantity of coke so that you had to start all over again; or the very subtle one whereby, at opposite diagonal corners of the camp, you have a shallow trench dug out ready for the laying of a crazy-paving path in one corner, and an actually completed path in the other. Each day, with a low, four wheeled, hand drawn trolley, you have the stone dragged from one corner of the camp to the other for the path to be re-laid, and the wetter or hotter the weather the better. These were punishment fatigues. Squadron fatigues were a week of duty during which recruits did all the menial, grubby jobs that the regulars preferred not to.

I had two particularly memorable days. The first was at the officers' mess kitchen where I scrubbed greasy tins and generally cleaned and polished. At about eleven thirty on this particular morning I was entrusted with a special duty. Handing me a large, stainless steel pail, complete with lid, a sergeant instructed me to go to the camp butchers, which was up near the guardroom. Together with detailed directions as to its location he gave me a list of meat that I was to bring back. Naturally, I marched to my destination as smartly as was possible with a large bucket unbalancing me on one side. I was met by a most ferocious looking man, perfectly cast for the part. He gave me the distinct impression that, if I so much as stepped into his den, he would rapidly turn me into sausages. I stood at a safe distance outside as he fulfilled the order.

It was some little while before the butcher returned with a nearly full bucket, and orders for me not to waste any time returning to the kitchens. The bucket was considerably heavier for the return journey and every few paces I was passed by an officer going in the opposite direction. Each one of these required a salute, which was no easy manoeuvre, especially as I cracked my left calf with the weighty bucket every time. Halfway back I was stopped by an inquisitive squadron leader. He asked what I was doing and where I was heading and, on being told, looked into my pail to confirm the story. Satisfied that all was in order, he sent me on my way, not before I had executed another painful salute.

This conversation between the officer and myself had, unbeknown to me, been watched with growing misapprehension by the sergeant waiting for me; considering me overdue, he had come out to look for me and to give me the rough edge of his rasp-like tongue. He was in a jittery state when I eventually arrived.

"'Ere" he began. "What you been talking about? I hope you didn't tell him nothing."

"What was there to tell him, sergeant?" was my innocent inquiry.

"All I said was that I had been collecting meat for the officers' mess."

"Are you sure that's all you said?" he asked anxiously.

"Positive, sergeant. I just told him the truth."

Whereupon the sergeant called the various cooks and helpers to him.

"Bert, here's your two pound of sausage. John, that bit o' steak I promised your missus. These pork chops and liver are mine and Bill, more sausages for you. Better get them away right now in case he comes sniffing round asking questions."

I had been the courier for their extra rations. I was given the cold shoulder for the rest of the day and was glad when my duty was over. When I had had time to ponder the matter, I thought it would have been difficult to prove that I was stealing the meat because I had no outlet for it. I had no doubt that the sergeant would have disclaimed all knowledge of it. Greasy pots and pans were not the only dirty work we were required to undertake.

Even worse was to follow the next day. This time, my duty was at the squadron stores. In between sweeping it out, cleaning the windows and polishing where necessary, I did some fetching and carrying. Armed with a trolley, I made my way to the main stores to bring back to our mess a new bacon cutter. I was accompanied by the NCO from the squadron stores. We were shown where this rather heavy piece of equipment was standing and left to load it on the trolley. On the way out, the NCO took from the shelves some drinking glasses, a water jug, a condiment set and various other items, some of which he told me to carry in my pockets and the rest were put on the trolley.

“You take this lot carefully back to the squadron stores and wait for me there. I’ll catch you up in a minute."

Off I went, once again oblivious of the fact that I was being made use of. Although it was a fair haul, I was back at the squadron long before the NCO. I went up the steps into the hut and emptied the things from my pockets on to the table.

With still no sign of the NCO, I removed the glasses and other items from the trolley and put them with the other things on the table. At last I heard footsteps arriving but they belonged to a flight lieutenant. I leapt to my feet. He came over and examined the loot.

“These yours?" He asked.

“No, sir, I’m just delivering them here”

“Who is responsible for them then?"

But before I could answer the NCO walked in. He was clearly worried and turned extremely pale.

“What are these glasses and things doing here, sergeant?"

“Replacements, sir. “Could you excuse me, sir, but they are wanting this bacon slicer rather urgently at the mess."

“Carry on sergeant”

And away he went, apparently satisfied with the explanation. Once we were alone, the sergeant was beside himself.

“What did you set them things out on the table for? You could have got me into a lot of trouble."

I really had no idea at the time that the goods were stolen and, even now, I break into a cold sweat when I think what might have happened to me had I been accused of the theft. How very relieved I was when that week of fatigues came to an end.

My mother had expressed a wish to travel up from Norfolk to attend our passing out parade. I couldn’t think why and tried to dissuade her, but her mind was made up. I remember feeling ashamed that she should see me in such a place and reduced to a mechanical puppet, but last-minute preparations with never-ending spit and polish soon diverted my thoughts. Never one to keep people waiting, my mother arrived some time before we came under starter's orders. She was welcomed at the main gate and directed, but not ushered, to the parade ground. With plenty of time in hand, she decided to take an unscheduled detour. This was what I had feared. She wandered off to an area where a junior flight was being blasted by a particularly foul-mouthed instructor. Turning to flee, she was confronted by a similar group being subjected to a similar barrage. No wonder she was looking unusually pensive when I saw her as I came on parade.

No mistakes with review order this time, but suppressed hilarity at the makeshift band that accompanied the parade. As the reviewing officer walked along inspecting the ranks, one of the raspberry section was blowing subdued oompahs. Unfortunately he ran out of breath and the note died thinly as he came up for air. I reckon it was the same band that had mesmerised the dancers that night I was on guard.

Before I could tell my mother that I had been posted to Cranwell, wherever that was, I could see that there was something she had to say first. She straightway told me of her walkabout among the junior flights.

Turning to the flight sergeant, she said

“I walked round the camp this morning and I have never heard such foul, disgusting language.”

Turning to me my mother added

“I hope you didn’t let him talk to you like that!”

Miraculously the flight sergeant was lost for words; fortunately for me he no longer had any authority over me.

9. RATS AND OTHER HEALTH HAZARDS

There is nothing like a row of condemned accommodation huts to fire the enthusiasm of a national serviceman newly posted to his permanent station. That they had been declared unfit for human habitation in 1934 gave them an almost antique value, much appreciated by the colony of rats that had moved into the area to share them with us. When the colder weather set in and the rats began their move into winter quarters, inevitable problems were created as to exactly where the rats could be tolerated, bearing in mind that, officially, they did not exist. They had two methods of entry, one of which was to climb through a conveniently placed open window, and the other was to come up the pipes that carried the water away from the basins and floor of the washroom at one end of the hut. To counter these moves we could, in the first place, shut all the windows, a singularly unattractive proposition with twenty occasionally washed bodies nightly fermenting away like a human compost heap. In any case, as far as we were concerned, these very real figments of our imagination were not welcome. It is funny how uncharitable green, or duck-egg blue, young airmen could be.

Matters came to a head when Ginger, who unaccountably had red hair, was bitten. He had woken up during the night, something had scuttled away from his pillow and, when he went to shave in the morning he saw a rather nasty looking bite on his right cheek. Now, most reasonable people would accept that, if there were no rats as the authorities assured us, then you could not possibly get bitten by one. But Ginger was a complaining sort and so, having bundled a few essentials into his small pack, he hurried off to report sick.

“What's your trouble then laddie?" the M.O. curtly inquired.

“I’ve been bitten by a rat, Sir.”

“What utter nonsense. If you come here with a cock-and-bull story like that, wasting my time, when I could be out on the golf course, you’ll find yourself in serious trouble, Laddie. More likely you got into a brawl and got a punch in the face, which serves you right. Now be off with you and think yourself lucky I'm not putting you on a charge. A rat bite, indeed!”

Reassembled in the hut that evening, we listened sympathetically as Ginger recounted his appointment with the M.O. Accustomed as we were becoming to the attitude of the authorities to anyone who presumed to have a thought or idea in his head, we were, nonetheless, unprepared for this turn of events. It was eventually decided that, since no one believed us about the rats, we must furnish proof of their existence. We agreed that, after lights out, everybody would arm themselves with a missile and stay awake to help kill a rat. The windows on either side of the hut, with the exception of the one in the middle through which rats were known to have gained access, were all firmly secured. The man nearest the light switch at the top end of the hut sat on a chair, ready to turn on the lights, with his feet on the seat of the chair and his backside on top of the backrest.

For once, lights out was awaited with keen anticipation. Everyone took up their position and began the vigil. After an hour or so people began to fidget and complain until it was pointed out that no self-respecting rat would venture into such a noisy billet. We gave complete silence one more try and then we heard it. The unmistakable sound of a roaming rodent; the slight scuffling on the window-ledge and the quiet thud as he landed on the chair beside Ginger's bed. Then another thud as it landed on the floor. Action stations! The light was turned on, Ginger shut his window and the rat, bang in the middle of the floor, looked for an escape route.

What chance did it have against twenty armed men? A volley of boots was flung in its general direction, the inaccuracy of which was a poor tribute to our shooting instructors. After forty pairs of boots had been loosed off the rat had slowed down appreciably as it made for the far bottom corner.

"Don't trap it in a corner!" went out the warning, as one intrepid hunter made menacingly towards it with the coke shovel.

"It'll fly at your throat if you're not careful."

Undeterred, Ginger closed in for the kill and with an almighty blow absolutely flattened the rat with the shovel.

The very next morning Ginger reported sick again, this time with his small-pack in one hand and a brown paper bag in the other. He was confronted by the very same Medical Officer.

"Not you again! "exploded the M.O.

"Yes, sir."

"And what the devil's the matter with you this time? Bitten by another rat, I suppose."

"Yes, sir."

“Now look here, you stupid little man, I warned you last time you came whining up here trying to skive off your duties. Well this time you're not going to get away with it…”

While the M.O. was thus exercising his painfully inadequate command of the English language, Ginger placed the brown paper bag on his table and proceeded to tear it open, revealing the squashed rat.

“That's what bit me, sir. It is a rat, isn’t it?” Ginger blurted out.

The torrent of abuse streaming from the M.O.'s mouth dried up as though struck by some instant drought. He gulped, eyes bulging in horror and disbelief.

“Rat, of course it's a bloody rat. There's no telling what disease you might have picked from it. Let's look at that face of yours. That's a rat bite right enough. Must get that seen to straight away. Better keep you in for a day or two in case it turns nasty. Why the hell didn't you report sick before and tell somebody about these rats?"

“I did, sir, but I was told --”

“Never mind what you were told," the crimson-faced M.O. butted in," Let's get that bite seen to.”

That was all that was seen to, although no one else was bitten by a rat for the remainder of my mercifully short stay in that condemned hut.

This was my first, albeit indirect, contact with station sick quarters. My next, personal, encounter was much more agreeable. A veritable army of spots had encamped on my back, defying all my efforts to uproot them. I’d even tried washing. Nothing else for it but to seek medical advice, chastened though I had been by Ginger's experiences. Nursing fears that I might easily be on the verge of becoming the first man court-martialled for spots, I summoned up enough courage to report sick.

“What’s the matter with you, then?"

From Ginger's description I knew that it was not the rat man who confronted me.

“Spots, sir. Hundreds of spots."

"Whereabouts?" he said suspiciously.

“Shoulders and back mostly, sir.” I ventured.

“Strip your shirt off then, and let's have a look. Umm. Looks as though you've got a nasty crop of spots on your shoulders and back,” he diagnosed.

“Thank you sir," I muttered gratefully, “I knew you’d spot the trouble straightaway."

“You need some treatment," he went on. “I’ll give you a chitty to take to the radiotherapy sergeant."

If you did not already know it, Norfolk is by some way the finest English county and Norwich the most splendid city, and when two people who are equally convinced of this meet by sheer chance they form an immediate bond of friendship. And this is precisely what happened when I met this sergeant. I at once recognised his Norfolk accent and we were soon discovering our common acquaintances in our home county. Some while passed before we got round to my spots but, in due time, we did.

“You’ve got a nasty crop of spots, mostly on your shoulders and back," the sergeant volunteered.

“Really," I said, “and what can be done about it, do you think?"

"Ultra-violet's the answer. I’d like you to come for treatment three times a week on Tuesdays, Thursdays and Saturdays - first thing."

He must have seen the disappointment that clouded my face as he suggested the arrangement. Arrangement, did I say? Normally, when a sergeant gives you such an instruction it is an irreversible order, but this was no common-or-garden sergeant, this was a Norfolk sergeant whom I knew I could trust. Risking all, I explained.

“I always go home on a Friday and I was hoping that you could see me on that day so that I could miss weekly parades. And, of course, if I have to have treatment on Saturdays I shan’t be able to get home in time to watch Norwich City.”

I could see that I had hit a sensitive nerve centre and I felt really bad about taking advantage of the good nature of a fellow Norfolk dumpling.

“Tell you what. Why don’t we make it Mondays, Wednesdays and Fridays? The course lasts for six weeks. You start off with half a minute and go up in half minutes to a maximum of ten minutes. Keeps your Saturdays clear and no point in your going on parade with all those spots. Yes, that’s what we'll do, if that suits you.”

“That’s marvellous, and very kind of you.”

So, for the next six weeks I turned up at the appointed times to have a treatment which did wonders for my spots. The sergeant used to bring in two cups of coffee and we would chat over people and places that we knew. Sick quarters was not such a bad place after all.

....

One warm, autumn afternoon some five or six weeks later, I was playing football for whatever section I was deemed to be in. It was a league match, as I recall, and just after half-time I went up to head a ball, challenged by an opponent who accidentally nudged me as we went for the ball together. I came down awkwardly, landing in a rabbit scuff with all my weight on my left leg. My left ankle buckled and it was very painful. Helpful hands removed my left boot, which caused the outside of the ankle to swell visibly.

"No sense in mucking about with that," came the voice of the referee, "we must get him straight up to sick quarters."

With a willing helper on either side I was trundled up to the station hospital, a distance of some eight hundred yards. There was no one about when we arrived and my two supports eased me gently down into a chair before returning to the match.

Doctors' waiting rooms are distinctly impersonal, antiseptic places but they have nothing on their RAF nineteen-fifties-style counterparts. Graphic posters inquired about your freedom from unmentionable diseases, or gave you instructions about the action you should take if exposed to Colorado beetles. For light reading there were copies of station standing orders for the last three and a half years, and some absolutely riveting construction plans for the half-throttled biplane. So engrossed was I in this unexpected feast of literature that I failed to notice the officer enter the room.

“What are you doing here at this time of day? Don’t you know sick parade is at nine o’clock in the morning?”

It was the rat man.

Overwhelmed by this spontaneous display of sympathy for a stricken fellow man, I struggled with tears of emotion as I said.

“I’ve hurt my left leg rather badly."

“Where’s your small pack, eh? You know damn well you don't report sick without it but then I don’t suppose people like you ever read or take any notice of standing orders. Well I'm not examining you without it, especially in that muddy state. You don't come up here without observing the proper procedures. Probably nothing wrong with you anyway.”

And with that he walked out.

Left alone once more, I had to give careful consideration to my next move. It was a good four hundred yards to my billet which I would have to reach by hopping on my right leg. Better remove my other football boot first, before trying my impersonation of a wounded kangaroo. Thirty hops and then rest and I would soon be there. Once or twice I overbalanced slightly, thus putting some weight on my damaged ankle which responded with an excruciating protest of pain. The flight of stone steps up to my barrack room was the most difficult part, but at last I reached the safe harbour of my bed.

For some while I was alone in the billet, but some friends came in later on and helped me down to the bath block where a good soak removed the mud that had so offended the sensitive M.O. At around five that afternoon I turned in because the ankle was really giving me hell. At that stage I think I really believed that a good rest and a sound night's sleep would do the trick. I was wrong, for the next morning the swelling was considerably greater, the ankle extremely tender. Persuaded, or to put it more accurately, ordered by a quite kindly corporal in charge to report sick, I reluctantly made my way back to the hospital with the help of two friends.

Guess what I did first, though? Yes, that's right, I put essentials into my small-pack and a copy of the rodent operative's manual to ingratiate myself to everybody's favourite M.O.

With that piercing stare and barking voice that passed for compassion, the M.O. eyed me as the usual itinerant malingerer. At least it was not ratty.

“I hope you haven't come to waste my time like the last airman," he blasted, an opening gambit perfected through years of contact with men bringing to him the guilt of their sickness. I wondered if I had done the right thing at all in coming to see him and was certainly willing to forego the experience of being treated to his bedside manner. Perhaps he had been frightened by a zeppelin as a young boy, I mused, and was getting his own back.

“Well? He shouted, interrupting my thoughts.

“Er, I hurt my ankle rather badly yesterday afternoon playing football. “

“Haven't you forgotten something?"

“Oh yes, we lost three one."

“No, you fool. It is customary to address a commissioned officer as sir."

" Oh yes, SIR, I'm sorry............SIR. “

"Well it’s your own stupid fault for playing such a ridiculous game. Might as well have look at your so-called injury while you’re here.”

He is bound to amputate, I persuaded myself, as I presented my offending ankle for inspection. With a firm prod of the index finger of his right hand he established beyond a reasonable doubt that my ankle was not only very swollen but also uncomfortably tender. Marvelling at his perception and keen powers of diagnosis, I asked.

“Is it broken, sir?”

“Shouldn’t think so from what you’ve said but we’ll have it x-rayed just in case. You’ll have to stay in for a week or so. Now, cut along and have a bath while I arrange a bed for you.”

He had certainly mellowed once he had convinced himself that I was the genuine article.

It was not at all bad in the hospital; the food was very good by military standards and the nurses were delightful, and delighted, to have a customer. They did not have all that many patients. They, like everybody else on the camp, were under additional pressure because, on the Friday of that week, there was to be an additional A.O.C’s inspection – the only one I ever experienced, and for which a little explanation is needed. A.O.C is Air Officer Commanding and inspection is painting, mending, washing and polishing everything, with a week of feverish activity preceding the fateful day. If that were not bad enough in itself, a far more severe blow was dealt to all national servicemen about a week before the actual inspection. It was announced that the length of service for conscripted men was to be increased forthwith from eighteen months to two years, and that everyone, except those with just a few weeks to serve, must remain for another six months.

Thanks to my mother, I was not affected by this new order because she had seen to it that I was entered for university before my national service began and I had already accepted a place. Still, I needed to confirm my lucky escape and sent off letters immediately, the replies to which quickly returned to assure me that my arrangement would be honoured. Others were not so lucky and the two or three of my friends who sent off university applications the moment the news was announced were disappointed. So was the patient in the bed two down from me. He missed being released by some four weeks and, having already become 'demob happy,' was faced with the prospect of another seven months' service. To say he was bitterly upset would do a gross injustice to the stream of expletives released by him at regular intervals for the rest of the week. What he was going to say when the A.O.C. came round would pin back every officers' ears permanently. They certainly weren't going to get away with curtailing his freedom in this way. We looked eagerly forward to the barrage of abuse that he promised to direct at our Air Officer Commanding, who was not a bad sort, actually.

My friends could only visit me briefly because they were required for a succession of 'bull-nights' and I became increasingly aware how fortuitous my injury had been. I was missing all the spitting and polishing currently being endured by practically all the other airmen on this huge camp. One friend popped in on the Wednesday to tell me a heart-rending tale. A bloke who worked in the kitchens had booked out some weeks back for a long weekend with his case full of Air Force bacon, butter and cheese, at a time which unfortunately coincided with a random check on cases. He had been sentenced to twenty-eight days in the 'glass-house' at Colchester. One of the things required of him there had been to scrub off all the blanco from his packs and webbing, right back to the bleached canvas. Because he was a model prisoner, he was given eight days remission of sentence, which in normal circumstance would have brought him joy and relief. What a shock for him to return to Cranwell to find that he had thirty-six hours to apply numerous coats of blanco to his kit to get it up to standard for the Friday!

At about eleven o'clock on inspection day, the Great Man appeared in the doorway of our ward, resplendent in all the trappings of an Air Commodore's uniform. I was still in bed and had been instructed to come to recumbent attention should the A.O.C approach me. Like a bee returning to the hive, he made unerringly for the disgruntled airman two beds down from me. We waited for the promised explosion.

"And what brought you into hospital?" the A.O.C. inquired.

"Ingrowing toenails, sir."

"Sorry to miss this morning's splendid parade weren't you?"

"Oh yes sir. Very sorry sir."

"And what do you think of the extra six months, eh?"

This was it. Ears and eyes strained to see the A.O.C. swept aside by the verbal broadside. Then the reply.

"It's all right sir. No bother, really."

"Nice to know that you people have taken it in your stride."

And with that he moved regally away.

My own officer came to see me just after I was allowed to get up for the day and I am sure that it was he who saw to it that I got the only official seventy-two hours pass I ever received, to complete my convalescence.

"Don't know what half the figures mean, Morrison, but I've sent off the weekly return. Be glad to have you fit again."

It was nice to know he meant it.

10. TURKEYS

Early December 1950 – Friday evening. It was five o'clock before I left camp and there was very little traffic. When I finally reached Norwich, it was half past ten - too late to catch the last bus. I phoned my mother and set off at a fairly brisk marching pace. By the time I reached the outskirts of the City at Harford Bridges, where the road forks left for Ipswich and right for my road (to Bury St Edmunds), there was no traffic at all. It was a fine, slightly frosty, starlit night.

A little before 1 a.m., I was just beyond Wreningham and approaching Ashwellthorpe. Except for an occasional owl to-whitting (but certainly not wooing), I had neither seen nor heard any person or vehicle for over two hours. Then, a policeman, the local bobby, emerged from the shadows. Remember, I was in RAF uniform with my small pack on my back.

"What are you doing here at this time of night?" he asked.

"I'm on my way home", was my obvious reply, as I recovered from the fright he had given me.

"What have you got in that pack?"

"Just some clothes that I'm taking home to be washed", I volunteered.

“I’d like to search your bag myself”, he demanded. So I unhitched my pack and stood by as he physically confirmed what I had told him.

“I expect you’ll want to know why I’m searching you like this.”

Well, I thought, I could be facetious and say that, for some time, I had expected people to be lying in wait, ready to pounce on me. Instead, I said

“Yes. I had wondered what you were up to.”

He then explained that a nearby farmer had had his turkeys stolen that night, and he had thought that I might be concealing one in my small pack!

The policeman went on:

“You said you were on your way home. Where exactly is that?”

“I live in Tacolneston with my mother and my grandfather, Joe Austin”.

“Old Joe Austin?” he exclaimed. “Your grandfather? How is he? Give him my regards!”

Then he looked at his watch, reminded me how late it was and asked me why I wasn’t hurrying home. Which of course I would have been, had he not jumped out on me and insisted on searching through all my dirty underwear. Not to mention that no self-respecting Christmas turkey would have fitted into a pack twice the size of mine.

Uncannily, almost ten years later, in the winter of 1959, I was in between jobs and working on a farm near Brighton. My main source of warmth was still my trusty RAF overcoat. If I could get to Seven Dials by 6.15 a.m., I was guaranteed a lift in a minibus full of construction workers on their way to Crawley New Town. Unfortunately, on this particular morning, I missed my lift, and for a while, stood on the corner outside a large bank, hoping someone else would take pity on me. Having had no luck and anxious not to be late, I decided to walk and had gone no more than a hundred yards when a police patrol car pulled up beside me; the officer in the passenger seat stepped out and asked me to get into the back seat of the car. He then asked me what was in the small case I was carrying.

"A Cornish pasty, some sandwiches, a piece of cake and an apple.... and a thermos flask of tea."

He opened the case and searched it. The driver then asked his colleague,

"What's he got in there?"

"A Cornish pasty, some sandwiches, a piece of cake and an apple.... and a thermos flask of tea."

Silence.

The officer sitting next to me said,

"I expect you're wondering why we stopped you?"

"Yes, I did wonder ....."

"Last night, the bank that you seemed to be loitering outside was robbed and we thought your case might be concealing some of the money that was stolen."

Déjà vu… another 'turkey' for the police!

They asked me where I worked – and seemingly satisfied with my response, offered me a lift the rest of the way. I arrived just in time for my seven o'clock start.

11. SALUTING

In our early days as recruits, we had frequently been warned that we had better watch our steps closely at all times. At some time during a given day, we were bound to break one of the million petty rules, often because we didn't know about them, and sooner or later someone in authority would catch us and make us pay. Our corporal at West Kirby had boasted: - "If I could follow you lot round all day and watch you all closely I'd have every one of you for something every day."

We didn't doubt it.

Ignorance of the regulations, you see, was no excuse. Doing absolutely nothing at all might, in itself, constitute an offence. You could be sure that if someone wanted your blood he could have it on the slightest pretext. Rather like the model recruit in the army, who completely exasperated his sergeant-major for not laying himself open for punishment. He was perfect, which made the sergeant-major even more determined to get him. After weeks of waiting, the sergeant-major saw his chance. The recruit was, legitimately, entering the camp on a bicycle. As he approached the main gate, he stopped pedalling and began to freewheel to a halt. He was charged and punished for "idling on a bicycle!"

It became really difficult when, knowing a rule and carrying it out to the letter, you were told that you were in the wrong. Remember that, in the end, superior rank wins any disputed point, as I was to discover.

The ground floor of the headquarters building at Cranwell had long, dark, narrow corridors. The connecting passages were in the centre, with rows of rooms on either side and when all the doors were closed, as they usually were, the only light was from dim electric light bulbs, widely spaced. It was virtually impossible to walk two abreast and when you met someone coming from the opposite direction, one of you had to turn sideways to allow the other to pass. What made it even more complicated was that the majority of people you encountered were officers, who therefore had to be saluted. This could be both dangerous and painful. Following one or two nasty clashes, the rules of procedure within the corridors were amended and duly printed on station orders.

In future, on entering the building, an airman would remove his headdress and tuck it under the flap on his shoulder. On encountering an officer, he would no longer be required to salute but would, instead, wish him good morning or whatever was appropriate. For once, I actually read this on orders and so acted accordingly. All went well for a couple of weeks and then one morning I found myself in trouble. I took off my hat as I came in at the rear entrance, walked briskly past the SWO's office before turning at a right angle to negotiate the long passage that led to my room at the far end. In the very dim light, I could see that the person coming towards me from that end was an officer. As we drew level I wished him good morning and continued on my way, quite unprepared for what followed. I had only gone a few paces when the air was pierced with an angry shout.

"AIRMAN – come back here."

"Yes, sir?"

"Haven't you forgotten something?"

"I don't think so, sir."

"Is it not customary to salute a commissioned officer?"

I could now see that I was in real trouble because I was confronted by a wing commander, legendary for his bad temper and intolerance. He was something to do with stores or transport and was quite objectionable. Once again I was struck by the differences between the superb officers on flying wing, pilots who taught the cadets to fly, and the bureaucrats and administrative officers who lived constantly in their shadow. The pilots had nothing to prove as to their courage and ability and their desk-bound counterparts had nothing much they could prove by comparison. Their frustration was understandable, but it was uncomfortable to be on the receiving end of it.

I began to reply: -

"Of course it is customary to salute sir, but the rules have recently been altered. You are not supposed to salute in these narrow corridors now because it is dangerous."

Even in the appalling light it was possible to see him turning purple.

"Don't you dare start quoting orders at me, laddie, or I'll have you marched off to the guardroom immediately."

"I'm sorry sir."

"Sorry. Sorry's not enough. Now, put your hat back on or I shall have you for being improperly dressed."

By this time, several doors along the corridor had been inched open to observe my discomfiture and this bellowing maniac. I began to move on again to my original destination. He grabbed me by the arm, beside himself with fury.

“Go back to the corner at the other end.”

Like some chastened schoolboy, I hurried to the corner.

“Now turn round, put your hat straight and come back here.”

I realised how important it was not to make the slightest false move, otherwise I would have burst out laughing. By now, I was once again level with the wing-commander.

“Now salute me, damn you,” he screamed. “What’s your name?”

“Morrison, sir.”

“You’re a marked man, Morrison. If ever you cross my path again and have the effrontery to quote orders to me I’ll have you locked up.”

It was quite alarming at the time, but I had come to no harm, although I had obviously made a dangerous enemy. So much for reading orders, for I was now totally confused as to what I should do if I should meet any other officer, who unbeknown to me, suffered from an inferiority complex, or who interpreted the new instructions in some other odd way. The matter was put to the test a fortnight later.

Various people had offered advice as to what I should do in a similar situation if confronted with the same man, provided that I recognised him soon enough. There was general agreement that no hard and fast rule applied because other officers might be just as upset to be given a salute after it had been specifically stated that it was not to be so. It was, in fact, a typical, no-win situation, as I discovered during a routine inspection. It was my turn to perform the duty of billet orderly for our room in one of the east camp barrack blocks. It was not long after ten, when, satisfied that all was presentable, I hurried downstairs to catch up with my weekly return before going home for the weekend. In the lower corridor, which was at least four times wider than the narrow tunnel in the headquarters building, the inspecting officer, a wing commander no less, with the usual entourage, was coming in my direction.

My hat was tucked under my shoulder flap. It was not my favourite wing commander; this one was a good deal larger but no less fierce. In the very short period available to make a decision, I favoured the safety of an each-way bet, which, at worst, could only be half wrong, and possibly doubly right. My beret was on my head in a flash so that, as the entourage drew level, I could whip off the smartest salute of which I was capable whilst at the same time offering a very polite good morning. Confident that my safety-first selection was a sure winner, I hurried on, just noticing the wing-commander turning for a sharp word to his aide. The aide, in turn, passed the word down the line until it had reached someone of a sufficient inferior rank to lower himself to address me.

“Airman,” was the original cry.

“Sergeant”, I flashed back, counting the three stripes in an instant.

“What the hell are you playing at?”

“I’m billet orderly this morning sergeant, and I am just returning to my section.”

“I’m not interested in that. Do you ever read orders?”

Checking the impulse to reply that I tried to avoid it wherever possible, I tried another tack.

“All the time sergeant. I almost know them by heart.”

“Really. Because you seem to have missed the one about saluting that came out about a month ago.”

“Not at all sergeant. I am only too well aware of it.” I then launched into my well-practised story. “And so you see, sergeant, I really don’t know what to do. With a wide corridor like this I thought I would cover both possibilities. What’s your advice?”

“My advice laddie, is to do what it says on orders. The wing commander was pretty annoyed and is expecting you to be disciplined. In the circumstances I’ll let you off with a warning. Watch your step in future.”

‘Never a second without a third,’ is one of those infuriating sayings that always seems to come to fruition when things are going wrong, and so it proved. Saluting had become a sore point with me and because of my two bewildering encounters, it was something I could not wittingly forget to do. Failure to salute a commissioned officer was so rarely a deliberate offence as to be negligible. To be accused of it in quite unreasonable circumstances was really the final straw in the matter.

It was a fair walk from east camp up to the mess in west camp and on a cold, wet and windy spring morning, it was also a most uncomfortable one. With collars turned up and hats pulled well down, a friend and I battled our way against the bitter breeze sweeping across the airfield. It would have been about a quarter to eight as we went onto the barrack square where the junior entry from the College had their early morning drill. Fifty or so yards short of the mess, there was a building with a tall brick chimney that housed an incinerator, I believe. Behind the further wall of this building, completely hidden from our view until we were past him, was the officer in charge of the practice. He had probably had a rough night, and his temper could only have been worsened by the dreadful weather and by the fact that his squad was late on parade. He was only a flying officer but he was spoiling for a fight.

A particularly strong gust forced our heads deeper into our collars as we neared our destination. We passed the incinerator building at a distance of some five yards, talking to one another as we did so. We were totally unaware of this officer to our left. Evidently he shouted at us, but his words were swept away by the howling wind, so he rushed out from his shelter and grabbed us both. Furious by now, he accused us of deliberately ignoring him and demanded to know our names and numbers. These we gave him, and he duly recorded them as we tried to apologise, at the same time explaining that we had truly not seen him. Not in the least calmed by our genuine protests of innocence, he told us that we could expect to find ourselves on a charge. We, somewhat belatedly, saluted him before making our way to a gloomy breakfast. We knew that, if it came to a hearing, our word would not be accepted against that of an officer and, for several days we lived on tenterhooks. We heard no more of the matter and we did not bump into that particular officer again. Although we always took care to look across to the wall every morning, our right hands poised to spring to the very smartest of salutes.

There is always a lighter side to these things that gives balance to what is, or at least should be, a trivial matter. Saluting comes automatically after a few months, but at the very beginning it can be a worry. When being taught the correct way at West Kirby, (longest way up, shortest way down), we had also been given instruction on how to recognise commissioned officers from our own and foreign forces. A few red herrings were thrown in as well just to keep us on our mettle. So, our corporal would say:

"Brigadier-general approaching your post, to the front salute."

And we would respond with the best salute we could muster, the higher the rank mentioned the harder we tried.

Then he would shout: - "Salvation Army General approaching your post, to the front salute."

Some would fall into the trap, some not. Even cinema commissionaires were accorded the honour, in the excitement of the moment, whereupon a broadside of amused scorn would pour from the instructor. If in doubt, salute was the policy I adopted when on my own in Norwich. I think that I had been brainwashed along with all the others into believing that failure to salute at the proper time would bring far more dire consequences than was actually the case.

So it was that, a mere seven weeks after beginning my national service, I was making my way along Prince of Wales Road en route to Thorpe Station. The pavements were thronged with servicemen, many of them Americans on their way to the Regent Cinema. Coming in my direction, a hundred yards away, were two American officers, recognisable by their chocolate coloured uniforms. By the distant look of it they were of quite high rank.

I should have known better than to worry, because my mother had been in the American Red Cross during the war and I had learned that they had a far more tolerant attitude to their men than did the British. Even so, I gathered myself to give an extra special salute, despite the fact that numerous American airmen ahead of me failed to even acknowledge their own officers.

The moment was upon me. Yes, they were two very high-ranking officers in the United States Air Force, only yards from me now. Perhaps this was the each-way bet that my brain had flashed to me that morning in the barrack block, for I saluted vigorously as I said:

"Good evening, sirs."

For a moment I thought they had not heard or that, maybe, they were ignoring me, but then the one nearest to me momentarily stopped chewing his gum to allow his jaw to sag in disbelief. He then resumed chewing, his hands thrust deep in his pockets. The officer on his inside was equal to the moment, for, after only the slightest hesitation he withdrew his right hand from his pocket and, making a circular motion with it, drawled: "Hi, buster" with just a hint of gratitude in his voice, as though recalling some long-faded memory.

So much for a high-ranking American officer approaching your post, I thought.

12. MISSING ITEMS

Three times a day we would make our way to the mess, (most appropriately named I always thought) for our meals. Food was still not in plentiful supply, nor were good cooks, in an airman's mess. We were more fortunate than many RAF camps, in that we had a NAAFI club at Cranwell where some reasonable food could be bought in the evenings. Because we were permanently short of money, we mostly had to rely on mess food to keep us going, food that with just a bit more thought and care could have been made much more palatable. On one occasion we had onions with our lunch and the following morning the porridge tasted strongly of them, no doubt because both had been prepared in the same vessel, which was not properly cleaned in between. In the middle of the summer we were once served watery tinned tomatoes for forty-two consecutive meals: breakfast, lunch and tea, living as we did in the horticultural heartland of England, where they could hardly give fresh tomatoes away.

The mess itself invariably reeked of stale food and the system whereby your knife, fork and spoon had to be dipped in a communal trough of hot water before you left was not the most hygienic of arrangements. It was one of my least favourite places and I had good reason to dislike it. During my week of compulsory duty in the cookhouse, at a time when I had begun to feel that the worst pitfalls had been avoided, I was sharply reminded how vulnerable my lack of rank made me.

At lunch one day, I was given the job of serving out the chips to the men, chips being a considerable luxury at the time. My strict instructions were that each man must be served one shovel-full only, although I might be tempted to give my friends extra. I could not be expected to pile exactly the same number of chips on to every plate, but I did my level best to make them equal. I thought I was doing it very fairly, until I was confronted by a corporal with whom I had never had any previous contact. As he presented his plate I shovelled a fair portion of chips onto it and prepared to serve the next man in the queue. The corporal did not move on but, standing his ground, challenged me:

"You've given me a short measure," he growled.

"You've got one shovel-full, the same as everybody else."

"I'm not moving until you give me a full portion."

"I'm sorry, but I can't let you have any more."

As I spoke, I cleared up two or three chips that had dropped from the metal dish on to the hotplate. Suddenly the corporal went berserk.

"I'm reporting you to the orderly officer for trying to serve me with chips that have been on the floor."

I had not attempted to put the chips from the hotplate on to his plate, but he must have thought that I was about to.

"I'll have you put on a charge for this," he screamed and had worked himself into quite a state when the officer arrived.

We were both interviewed separately, and I was keenly aware that my word would not be accepted against that of the corporal.

I think the only reason the matter was allowed to drop was that the corporal could not bring himself to speak civilly to the officer, who would normally have backed two stripes against none. That was not altogether the end of it, however, because the obviously vindictive corporal came back to me, after the officer had left, to threaten me.

"Don't think you'll get away with this. I'll fix you one of these days, don't you worry."

I never again got within range of that particular corporal but a few weeks later he came into the mess with his face severely rearranged. His lips were puffed up and cut, both his eyes had been blacked and he had various cuts and abrasions on the rest of his face. I cannot honestly say that I was either surprised or sorry to hear that he had provoked an argument with another airman, a good deal more belligerent than myself, who had ultimately waylaid him and punished him for his unpleasantness. Unfortunately, the attacker was identified and brought to book for attacking the corporal with a king-sized chip on his shoulder.

Not long after this, I had an even more unpleasant experience connected with the mess. It was a cold, rainy day as I prepared to walk over to have my lunch. I would need to put on my overcoat; I could have done with my groundsheet as well, but it was in my locker way down on east camp. Buttoned up against the driving rain, I hurried across to the mess and hung my coat in the cloakroom before going in for my lunch. The meal over, I went to collect my overcoat from its peg. There were hundreds of pegs, so I didn't know the exact one my coat was hanging on. After a good search I couldn't find it, so I waited for everyone to finish, thinking that the one coat that then remained was bound to be mine. The last few stragglers went out and there were no coats left. All the pegs were empty.

I went straight up to the guardroom to report my coat missing. The service policeman at the desk, another corporal, was extremely sceptical about my story.

"It's quite common for people like you to make up such a story to avoid being punished for losing their overcoat. I don't believe a word of it. Where did you say you left it?"

"In the cloakroom of the airman's mess, but it's not there now."

"That's what you say. I'm going to look and you're coming with me."

Off he went back to the mess on our fruitless journey.

"Are you sure you were wearing it when you went to lunch?" I was asked. Yes, I was absolutely sure, and I was also sure that the coat was marked with my number, which the corporal also doubted.

He wrote down my name and number so that the loss of my coat could be printed on orders the next day. He also warned me that if my coat was not found by the end of the week I would be in trouble, court martial and all that. It sounded a bit heavy-handed and unlikely to me, but I had no means of knowing what would happen. I heard nothing for three days and my feeling was that the longer it went on, the less likely was it that the coat would turn up. Not only that, but it was absolutely essential that I have it for hitch-hiking home on the Friday. I would freeze without it.

At about eleven on the Thursday morning the telephone in my flying wing office rang. It was the guard room informing me that they thought my coat had turned up and I was to report to them at once. I lost no time in hurrying to the guard room.

"Where is it then?"

"Where you left it, of course."

"I'm not sure I understand."

The corporal got up from his desk:

"Come over to the mess with me and you'll see exactly what I mean."

We walked over to the mess and there, on a peg very close to where I had originally hung it on the Monday, was an overcoat. Inspection of the number printed on the white inner lining showed it to be the one that I had had stolen.

"That's it," I said, greatly relieved.

"Exactly where you left it, eh? Next time make sure you look more thoroughly before you waste our time. It's most likely been here all along."

"Look here, you know that's not true, the place was empty when you searched." I protested.

"Don't take that attitude with me, laddie, or you'll be in more trouble than you bargained for."

I bowed to the inevitable. It didn't take a great deal of working out. Somebody without a coat had made off with mine and had either seen orders and feared a kit check or had thought better of it.

The main thing was that I was reunited with my coat and that was all that really mattered, plus getting away from the guardroom…

I never understood why it was that all service policeman, without any exception whatsoever, found it necessary to be unapproachable and objectionable at all times. Imagine a local policeman doing nothing but rousting and threatening the members of his community with whom he was obliged to come into contact, and completely ignoring all the others. Even when you went to the guardroom for advice or a weekend pass, you were treated with suspicion and hostility, so that the idea of ever co-operating with them, even in a good cause, was unthinkable. Furthermore, any opportunity to cast them in an unfavourable light was eagerly seized upon. On one such occasion, the cadets at the college came face to face with this formidable foe.

Each year, the Cranwell sports teams met their opposite numbers at Sandhurst in sporting combat. It was always the highlight of the season. The Cranwell rugby fifteen had been away to Sandhurst and lost their game by eight points to nil. The subsequent after-match drowning of sorrows had led to a small group of the air cadet rugby team 'borrowing' one of the ceremonial cannons from their army hosts and towing it back to Cranwell under cover of darkness. In due course, the people at Sandhurst discovered their loss, quickly put two and two together, and phoned through to us to say that they suspected our rugby players of the theft. The guard room went earnestly into action, searching every unlikely place the length and breadth of the entire camp. They were baffled. The cadets had actually tethered the cannon to the flagpole in front of the main college building, covering it with a tarpaulin. It was so obvious that the police missed it until, after hours of fruitless searching, it was discovered. Hot on the scent now, the police lumbered in for the kill. It was narrowed down to a particular under-officer who was classically interrogated by an intrepid guard room corporal. With pencil licking thoroughness he wrote.

"I approached the under officer and said, 'I am charging you with being in improper possession of a cannon!' He made no reply." Could he really have been expected to follow that?

At the subsequent inquiry, it was decided that the four cadets largely responsible for removing the cannon from Sandhurst should be provided with a three-ton lorry with which they would return the stolen article to the place from which they had removed it. It was generally anticipated that our cadets would get a very rough welcome when they got there. To make sure, the Sandhurst cadets were advised of their arrival. In the event, the four culprits received a heroes' welcome and returned even more befuddled than the first time. The last entry on the evidence file was a large sheet of paper on which were written just three words: - "Jolly good show."

I would like to think that the four enterprising cadets responsible for the prank got the early promotion they deserved.

13. FIRE!

Everyone had to spend a week as a fire picket while at their permanent station. I was no exception, because this was one of the few things that my connections on the inside could not fix. There was a master list somewhere that no one could alter. Thus it was that I was summoned for duty - and what a memorable week resulted. We reported to the fire section first thing Monday morning, to be met by a surprisingly amiable, veteran fireman, with well over twenty years of going to blazes under his belt. Having stressed to us the importance of remaining in the section at all times except for meals, he then showed us to our quarters. Opening the door into a dim, tatty and rather airless room, he announced: -

"This is your base for the next week lads. Make yourselves comfortable." There was a direct contradiction here because, with the dilapidated room as our home, there was not the slightest possibility of being comfortable. However, we were left to our own devices for the rest of the morning, being on standby in case of emergency. Any fire that we had been called to at that stage of the proceedings would certainly soon have become an emergency, but by the evening we had gained valuable experience.

Shortly after we returned from lunch our friendly corporal put his head round the door to ask: -

"Shall we pop outside for a bit of training lads?"

It was a beautiful sunny day, which made it all the more claustrophobic in our temporary billet, so we were very pleased to have the chance of stretching our legs outside. We were led towards a lean-to shed, housing what appeared to be the prototype of Boadicea's chariot. It was in reality a hand-drawn hose reel, which was flanked by two enormous wheels with an extended wooden T-bar to pull it. It was the most sophisticated piece of firefighting equipment we encountered during the whole week and our corporal was obviously attached to it.

"This is a reel of hose," he informed us, and before we could begin to express astonishment, he excited us with the prospect of learning how to use it. Bear in mind that the hose was of a considerably earlier vintage than our corporal. He wondered which of us would like the privilege of pulling it over to the hydrant in the middle of the barrack square. We all pressed eagerly forward to be one of the favoured two given this enormous responsibility. For once I was lucky and with a sense of absolutely no pride whatsoever, I helped to pull the ramshackle reel to the hydrant.

Things now became really complicated. The corporal began by allocating us our various duties in a most civilized fashion, whereby he asked if we would like to do the job rather than curtly ordering us. Two men would be at the nozzle end, one would be the runner to convey the orders to another chap and myself at the tap end. We ran out the ancient length of hose before gathering round for final instructions.

"The runner will be at the nozzle end with me. I shall shout to him the order 'water on', whereupon he will run down to you two at the hydrant and shout – 'water on.'"

With some difficulty we then connected the hose to the hydrant, after which the corporal went on: -

"Now, although we have connected the hose, this is only a practice so when I says 'water on' you don't actually turn it on, you just repeat the message and stand where you are."

As we marvelled at the subtlety of it all it became even more hilarious.

"The runner then runs back to me and waits until we've put the fire out. At this point I gives him the order 'water off' and he runs down to the hydrant and repeats 'water off.'"

We were ahead of the corporal as he continued: - "Now, as you hadn't actually turned the water on you won't be in a position to turn it off, will you? Sorry to make it so complicated for you lads at the hydrant. All ready to give it a go? Take up your positions then."

Away we went. The runner was given the order and trotted down to us to give his instructions. We did nothing. He trotted back, we waited, and he eventually came with the order to turn the water off. We did nothing. The corporal beckoned to us to gather round, a kindly smile on his wrinkled face. Fighting back tears of emotion, he gulped: -

"You know lads, that's the finest first practice I've ever seen. I'm proud of you. Would you all like to go through it again?"

"Ooh, yes please corporal," we cooed in unison.

"I thought you might," he confided. "Let's do it a bit faster this time. Anybody want to change jobs?" Nobody did.

I looked at my friend and he at me.

"Shall we?" I inquired hopefully.

"Why not."

The men at the nozzle braced themselves as the runner, sprinting this time, arrived with the breathless message – "Water on."

We grabbed the turnkey and wound it frantically. It was too much for the hose that had not seen action for several years. It split in a dozen places as the water spurted everywhere. The only place lacking a jet was the nozzle because all the water had escaped before it reached that point. Soon the parade ground began to flood, and we wondered if we had done a dreadful thing. Faced with a new experience the corporal froze until, at last, he shouted into the runner's ear. Head thrown back with effort he raced to the hydrant yelling: - "Water off."

Sagely the two of us consulted and agreed that when he said water off we were to do nothing. Back went the runner only to return immediately: - "Water off." He screamed. Daring no further, we complied with the order.

By this time the whole parade ground was awash, the hose on the point of disintegration. The corporal wearily gathered us round him for the last time, choking on tears of disappointment. It was some time before he could bring himself to speak and with every passing second we imagined excruciating punishments.

"Sorry it ended like this lads. I'm going back to my bunk to have a rest. Roll the hose up and put it back in the shed." And with that he trudged sadly away and nothing more was said or done about the incident. We felt awful.

We did not have another practice, but we tried to make up to the corporal for our waywardness for the next few days, during which nothing at all happened. It was on the Thursday that things livened up considerably. One of the tasks that each of us had to perform was cinema duty. For one evening we made our way down from the west camp to the cinema at the east camp, there to sit through the films to be on hand to raise the alarm and to search the building at the end of the evening. People were liable to throw burning cigarette ends on to the floor and it was the fire picket's job to search for them and for any other potential source of fire to prevent the place from going up in smoke. It also had the advantage for the authorities that, in the event of a fire, the man on duty from the fire section could be blamed for it, no matter how thoroughly or conscientiously he may have carried out his search. Apportioning of blame was the official description of it. Scapegoat was the truer definition.

Thursday was my night at the cinema. Putting on my red arm-band, which we had to wear at all times during the week, I set off for what turned out to be a most amusing night's work. The fire picket sat in a special seat at the end of a row some two thirds of the way back from the screen. At about eight o'clock the manager tapped me on the shoulder: -

"You are the fire picket, aren't you?"

"Yes, is anything the matter?"

"There's a fire out at the back," He answered without any great urgency in his voice.

"Not in the cinema?" I whispered, scrambling to my feet.

"Oh No." He reassured.

I hurried to the back of the cinema, following the manager outside through the back door. There, several hundred yards away, were the unmistakable signs of a fire. Using the telephone in the manager's office I rang straight through to the fire section. The suddenly woken voice from the other end said, blearily:

"Fire section."

"Ah", I blustered, "There's a huge fire near the…"

"Have you put the emergency drill into operation?"

"No, but you see there's this fi-"

"It's no use until you've been through the official drill."

"But you don't understand there's this fire near the petrol-"

"Put down the 'phone and get the exchange. Give them your name and tell them to alert the emergency services, then ring me back." And he put down the 'phone.

I at once got on to the exchange to tell them to put the emergency fire procedure into operation and then asked them to put me through again to the fire section.

"'Allo, fire section."

"It's me again, about this huge fire in.."

"What's your name?"

"What has my name got to do with it? Look.."

"I got to fill in the official form first in case it's a hoax. Name?"

"Name? Oh, Morrison. Now look here.."

“Number?” He persisted.

“Number? Number of what?” was my puzzled reply.

“Your service number.” I do not now remember what that number was, but I gave it to him.

“This fire is in a potentially dangerous place,” I rattled on.

“What section are you in?”

“Oh, for goodness’ sake, get on with it.”

“Don’t you take that tone with me, laddie. I want to know your section and the name of your section commander.”

To my utter disbelief, this went on and on, although he did not want to know what size shoes I took. Finally, he asked: -

“Now, about this fire.”

“I shouldn’t bother,” I grunted sarcastically, “it’s probably out or out of control by this time.”

“Watch it, laddie. You’re wasting valuable time!”

Over five minutes had elapsed since my original call but eventually the message got through. No Wells Fargo rider ever had a more difficult passage than this. Putting down the ‘phone, I was left yet again to marvel at this pettifogging red-tape to absolve themselves of any responsibility. The sort of thing, up with which Winston Churchill quite rightly would not put.

After a word with the manager I resumed my seat in the cinema. The film was over just before eleven. I checked every row most carefully, before informing the manager that I had satisfied myself that all was well and that I was going back to the fire section.

It was a beautiful night as I strolled back to the billet, marred only by the laboured drone of Harvard aircraft as they lanced into the darkness on their night-flying training. Somebody was bringing me some grub back from the NAAFI, which I was looking forward to eating before turning in. I even persuaded myself that the billet was not that uncomfortable compared with, well, something. It was unusually quiet as I approached a door, for they could not all be asleep, I thought. There was a stony silence as I went in to what looked like a casualty clearing station. Before I could put my own question, someone asked: -

“Was it you who ‘phoned up about the fire?”

Not fully realizing the significance of the inquiry, I answered honestly.

“Yes. Nothing wrong is there?”

“Wrong,” everyone shouted back, and then their spokesman retold the nightmare for my benefit and discomfort.

Putting down the ‘phone after extracting my life history, the NCO in charge that evening threw open the fire billet door shouting,

“Fire!”

The room was deserted. No one had even bothered to shove a pillow down a bed to give the appearance of occupation. A second shout of fire died on the NCO’s lips as he searched the rest of the building in vain. No luck. After a moment’s thought he made his way over to the NAAFI where he found a small, but lively party in progress. One of the fire pickets was celebrating his birthday in style with everyone by this time well over the limit.

"Come and have a drink with us," he called to the onrushing NCO.

"If you aren't back at the section in one minute flat I'll put you all on a charge," came the friendly reply.

It wasn't possible for two of the temporary firemen to make their own way back to base without assistance and, in fact, the NCO half carried, half dragged one across the square. Awaiting this shaky crew was a small pick-up truck with a canvas hood over the back, already loaded with picks and shovels. The men were bundled roughly into the back where they could not sit down because of the tools littering the floor. However accomplished a firefighter the NCO might have been he was no prize winner as a driver. Starting the engine impatiently, he revved up furiously as he threw the vehicle into reverse. Lifting his foot suddenly from the clutch, he took the unsteady crew completely off guard flinging them violently to the floor, there they landed heavily on a pick or shovel, inflicting upon themselves sundry cuts, bruises and tears in their clothing. Intoxicated curses filled the air as they struggled to regain their feet but it was not to be, as the driver trod on the brake, causing them all to lurch to the front. Almost at once the truck leapt forward in first gear, hurling them to the floor once more. Each change of gear produced another crisis at the rear, as did the violent swerves at each turn and the fierce braking at the T-junction by the guard-room. Once on to the main road the tangled heap again began to unravel itself, by this time badly bruised, shaken and torn. Whatever the inferno they were rushing towards, the firefighters in the truck would scarcely be able to stand upright, never mind tackling a raging fire.

The driver had one further trick up his sleeve. As he whizzed recklessly down the road he looked to his left and spotted the fire across a field. Seeing a gap in the hedge, he simultaneously touched the brakes and yanked the steering-wheel over to the left. The deepening chaos at the back took on another dimension as the vehicle bounced crazily on the uneven surface of the field. No one made any further attempt at getting up as they were jolted cruelly from pick to shovel. They had become too battered to shout their unheeded complaints at the frenzied driver. He was surely extracting sweet revenge for that empty billet and that NAAFI party, but there was further humiliation ahead.

Once more he hit the brakes hard, bringing the truck to a sliding halt. Nobody attempted to move until the NCO leapt from his cab, shouting as he did so for the crew to look lively. Slowly, painfully, they fell out on to the field, the stubble of which had been burning a little earlier. But while that prolonged 'phone call was taking place, that empty billet was being discovered and the party broken up, other forces were being mobilized. A telephone call had alerted the civilian fire brigade at Sleaford. They were on the road in a trice, homed in on the stubble fire in professional fashion and had it under control long before it could threaten the married quarters in its eventual path. As the RAF truck arrived the Sleaford engine was pulling away from another job well done.

Grieving inwardly, fuming outwardly, the NCO snapped: -

"There's no point in our staying here, lads. Jump back in so that we can hurry back to base just in case we are needed elsewhere."

Too weak to protest, the dazed men clambered clumsily into the back once more, only to be flung on their backs and on their faces, re-enacting the nightmare as the driver worked off his latest frustration. If possible, that return journey was worse than the outward run. At last the ragged rabble tumbled out in front of the fire section and made its way to the relative safety of the billet. They were too exhausted even to raise their voices at the unwitting perpetrator of their misery. I didn't dare to ask if anyone had brought me a drink and sandwiches.

14. TRAVELLING HOME

It's about ninety miles from Cranwell to Norwich, with King's Lynn almost exactly the halfway point, and along this route I hitch-hiked home some sixty times. It usually took me about four hours to cover the distance. Traffic was relatively light as far as King's Lynn, and on the odd occasion when I had to wait until Saturday, the absence of any lorry traffic made the journey very slow indeed. Occasionally, during the winter months, I would be late leaving on the Friday, only to find, understandably, that drivers were reluctant to pick me up after dark. On such nights, if I couldn't reach the Surrey Street bus station for the last bus home at nine-twenty, I would sometimes have to walk the last ten miles. I once arrived home at one-thirty after such an experience, to find, as always, that my mother had a roaring fire and a hot meal ready and waiting. One particularly filthy night, I had walked to within three miles of home when a car from the next village, driven by a friend of my grandfather's, picked me up. The driver could have made a detour past my house that would have taken him three minutes longer. I could not, of course, ask him to do so, and was disappointed when he turned off at Ashwellthorpe and dropped me almost as far from home as I was when he had stopped to pick me up.

The reason that I always made the journey home by getting lifts in this way was that I simply didn't have sufficient cash to buy a train ticket. That was the overriding consideration. There were added factors, like the remoteness of the camp and the fact that it didn't really matter whether the journey took two or six hours since I had no deadline to meet at the other end. It was different for the return, because I had to be back by a certain time which I could not overrun. It took three quarters of my week's pay to make the journey back to camp, a journey which I never once attempted to cover by hitch-hiking.

There were not that many vehicles on the roads but most of them would stop to pick up a man in uniform, very often because the driver had in his turn been grateful to people who willingly give him a lift when he was serving in the forces. I always wore my uniform and tried to make my way to the Sleaford road around lunchtime on the Friday. Considering the number of times I walked along that back road to get on to the main highway, it was little short of miraculous that I was never once seen, stopped or questioned by someone in authority and asked where I was going. I suppose anyone who did see me thought that I would not be such a fool as to make off in broad daylight without a valid pass. Many of the persons who might have been interested were, of course, usually having their lunch, but even so I led a charmed life. Once on the main road, it was imperative that I got an early lift, and this never failed to materialise. One of the earliest of these rather spoiled me for the rest of my time at Cranwell. A Rolls-Royce loomed into view barely a minute after I reached the top road. It was no more than a token gesture that I made with my thumb because I certainly did not expect such a magnificent vehicle to stop. But stop it did. Where was I heading? Norwich? That is where the Rolls-Royce was being delivered, to a dealer there. I sat back to enjoy the grandest lift I ever had. I was even treated to a meal on the way and was in Norwich just after three o'clock.

The only other Rolls that ever picked me up was in entirely different circumstances. My departure from camp had been delayed and by the time I set off at five o'clock, it was already dark. As usual, I got an immediate lift, which took me as far as Swineshead. This was by far the most frequent first pick-up, because many of the cars and lorries were on their way to Boston and they turned off at Swineshead. So there I was, in this bleakest of spots, as it began to rain. Experience quickly taught me that a combination of rain and darkness made drivers reluctant to stop. They did not see you until they were nearly upon you - and also they were not as likely to spot that you were in uniform. Anyway, an hour went by and what few vehicles there were showed no sign of stopping. I never stood still for long, so I must have walked at least a couple of miles before a car driver finally took pity on me. A superb, vintage Rolls-Royce coasted silently to a halt some forty yards ahead of me. I rushed towards it, to be greeted by a distinguished, elderly gentleman in evening dress. Looked as if I would be glad of a lift, he thought, on such a filthy evening. He and his wife were dining in King's Lynn and they would gladly take me there. Army man himself, colonel, who would always lend a helping hand to a stranded serviceman. His wife, resplendent in her evening gown and jewellery, sat magnificently erect in the back, holding firmly to a tassel-like support. We never exceeded twenty-five miles an hour as we progressed regally towards King's Lynn but I was relieved to be out of the driving rain. They dropped me at the Norwich turn, where once again I had a lengthy wait, so that by the time I got to Swaffham, my last bus was leaving Norwich. Fortunately, I was just in time to catch the theatres and cinemas coming out and a theatregoer gave me a lift to round off a trip that took nearly seven and a half hours.

At one stage in the spring, my routine had fallen into such a regular pattern that I was getting to King's Lynn at roughly the same time every week - during the middle of the afternoon. Early on in this period, I was offered a lift by a young man in his early twenties, driving an M.G. He whisked me into Norwich in no time at all. During the journey, he told me that he made this same trip each week at approximately the same time, and that if I could manage to be there, then he would always pick me up. True to his word, he did just that, but eventually I came to the conclusion that he drove rather too fast. He confirmed my belief during one frighteningly memorable trip. Only a few minutes after taking me on board, he was passed by a man on a high-powered motorbike. As he went by, the rider half turned his head in a somewhat contemptuous manner. A glaze came over the eyes of my M.G. driver as he set off in pursuit. Jaw set, foot thrust hard down, he swept majestically by the presumptuous motorcyclist, with what I took to be an air of inevitable finality. Not a bit of it. At a mere eighty miles an hour or so, the chase had scarcely begun in earnest. Opening up a notch or two, the rider ranged alongside, smiling, as though appreciating the contest he had provoked. As he made to pull away again, the motor cycle hesitated, puffing smoke from its exhaust. He dropped back and, leaning over sideways, appeared to be making some adjustment.

We were both held up at East Winch, where the two rivals chatted in friendly fashion, discussing the exact nature of the malfunction in the motorbike. Soon we were off again, with the same process repeated. At length the motorcycle rider overcame his problem and drew alongside the M.G. as the speedometer soared into the nineties. Pushing his car to the limit, until the needle wavered around the hundred mark, my companion in the car had to acknowledge defeat as the motor bike thundered by, drawing steadily clear. We were held up at the East Dereham level crossing, which our opponent had cleared, and we didn't see him again. I was enormously relieved that we made the remainder of the ride at a relatively modest speed. I had been petrified at times, although even this didn't turn out to be the most frightening moment of my hitch-hiking career.

It was at the beginning of the football season and my officer had asked me to see the CFI with him on the Saturday morning. That done, I followed the usual formula, whereby I would request permission to carry on up to headquarters building, and the officer would say that he would see me on Monday morning. I reached King's Lynn in average time, when a saloon car stopped and offered me a lift to Norwich. He was going to watch Norwich City and so was I. Things were going well until, of all things, we got stuck behind an RAF lorry. On board were a number of airmen, waving to us out of the back of the lorry. Try as we might, we could not overtake and as kick-off time drew closer, so did frustration increase. Still no opening. By this time, the boys in the back of the lorry were really enjoying themselves as they practised their greatly exaggerated Churchillian gestures. Somewhere near Narborough, my driver's patience snapped. With only a short stretch of clear road ahead, he pulled out to overtake. At that moment a small, red mail van swept round a corner and roared towards us. If the lorry driver had been prepared to give way by easing his foot off the accelerator, we could comfortably have cut in front of him, but he drove even faster. My driver was committed, level with the cab of the lorry. The mail van was upon us. I was sure that I was about to die. Helpless and scared, I waited for the end. Those three drivers must have felt the same, but they were all of them ice cool. Not one of them panicked, braked or attempted to take evasive action, which would have resulted in disaster. Instead they held to a straight course and, with inches to spare on either side, we passed without touching, three vehicles across a narrow road, with scarcely any verge. Shaken, the lorry driver now eased back and waved us past.

I was still wobbly when I got out of the car, having already decided to go straight home and give the football match a miss. Not many things would have kept me away from Carrow Road in those days, but that did.

Every new journey was begun in a mood of buoyant optimism. This would definitely be the day to surpass all days. That blue car coming up the hill only seconds after you got on to the road was going all the way to Norwich. In fact, you persuaded yourself, it would take you within spitting distance of your house. Out with the thumb for this outstanding lift. He swept by, in total disregard of your urgent signals, and empty at that. What a rotten... No, you couldn't expect to strike gold immediately. It was no good getting cross and, in any case, he probably was not going your way. A clapped-out lorry is approaching. Try to look disinterested, give no indication that you are actually hitch-hiking, and he'll go straight past. Good job he didn't stop; he was bound to be making for Norwich, taking ages longer than you usually took. Another promising looking car goes sailing by. You can't afford to hang about in this most vulnerable place, so you must lower your sights and hail whatever comes along. Another tired lorry wheezes up the hill, sees you and comes to a halt where you're standing: -

"I'm going to King's Lynn if that's any good to you, mate."

"Thanks very much, that'll be fine." And to think you turned your nose up at the last lorry. Most lorries were slow in those days, but so what? You were out of the danger zone, travelling in the right direction. With few exceptions, lorry drivers had been in one or other of the armed forces, so the time was spent comparing notes or listening to reminiscences. Most of the companies they worked for discouraged or even forbade the giving of lifts because of difficulties over insurance, but their drivers always waived the rule for a man in uniform. Although he told you he was going to Lynn, your driver might well be going beyond there in your direction; very often he would give the first place of any size that he was passing through, thinking his distant destination might be beyond your reckoning.

I had been waiting ages at Swineshead Bridge, not because scores of potential lifts turned me down, but because the road was unusually quiet. I had long since passed the stage of ignoring lorries, even a tandem bicycle would have been acceptable. At length, a lorry groaned into earshot. As it came into view, I could see that it was piled high with boxes. Slow but sure, if only it would stop. It did. On closer inspection, it was quite a new lorry, but the boxes were obviously full, which accounted for the straining noise of the engine. He was on his way to Norwich, if that would help. I leapt eagerly aboard, my worries over for the day. In fact, the lorry went quite fast; too fast, perhaps, in the circumstances, as the driver explained to me.

"These new lorries are all very well but where's your protection, eh?"

"Protection? Protection for what?" I asked.

“Look out of this front window and what do you see?"

Road was the only answer I could think of, but I was sure he didn’t mean that. Indeed, he might think I was trying to be funny and tip me out. I’m not sure if he expected an answer, but, before I could think of a satisfactory one, he went on:

"Give me a lorry with a bit of bonnet on it. Longer the better. Not like this thing, absolutely flat at the front. What do you think I'm carrying then?"

I was a little confused, not yet having connected the strong odour permeating the cab with the load at the back.

"Fish," he said. "Fifteen tons of fish. Now supposing I had to brake in an emergency because I was going to hit something. What do you think would happen?"

"New brakes, sharp reflexes, you'd stop in a matter of a few yards", I flattered.

"Aye, I might at that, but you and me’d be past caring." I was getting worried. "Why’s that, then?"

"Why? I'll tell you why. Just as much as touch anything with that flimsy front and it will cave in. And the back of the cab's no better. Like balsa wood it is. If I slap my brakes on in a hurry, that fifteen ton o' fish would come belting forward through the back of the cab and squash us like flies. I'm telling yer, you wouldn't stand a chance. Mind you, you wouldn't know much about it."

Fine consolation, I thought. I fretted for the rest of the journey. There I had been, reluctant to solicit a ride in a slow lorry that turned out to be not slow at all, only to wish that it not go so fast.

As we approached a sharpish corner at speed, I consoled myself that here at least there was no cause for alarm.

"Corners like this is the worst of the lot," he blurted out, as though reading my thoughts. "This is the worst balanced lorry I've ever handled. It'd tip over at the drop of a hat and then where would we be?"

Hospital, I thought, but didn't say it, as I watched the signposts flashing the mileage to Norwich. Not far now and soon there. It had actually been a very swift lift and I was grateful for it, though just as grateful to step down from the cab. I was just in time to catch the four twenty bus. Tea was cooking as I entered the front door. My father had brought home fresh fish from Lowestoft!

Going home, then, posed very few problems. Getting back was a different matter. Hitch-hiking was out of the question. For a time, a school-friend of mine from the same village was stationed at nearby Swinderby and he gave me a lift back on Sunday nights which was, of course, perfect, since he dropped me only a few hundred yards from my quarters. That arrangement lasted about four months, although it was by no means every week, because he didn't always come home. He drove a newish Austin van, mechanically excellent and never any trouble at all. We, or at least I, did have one alarm. It was a beautiful summer's evening and, as we came to the outskirts of East Dereham, I asked David if he would like an ice-cream. Although it was half past ten on a Sunday evening, there was a small sweet shop that was always open, where we had called frequently before. Ice-cream it was. I had made myself comfortable by not wearing my beret and by leaving undone the belt of my best blue tunic. We stopped outside the shop. No need to make myself fit for inspection, so I just hopped out of the van as I was and dashed in to buy the ice-cream. As I was emerging through the shop doorway, a voice screamed: -

"Airman, come here at once!"

Even before turning to look, I sensed that it was service police. I dashed over to the van as their renewed yells shattered the peaceful Sunday calm. They were seventy or so yards away and breaking into a run. David had seen what was happening and had the engine running. As soon as I was half-safely in, I shouted: -

"Clear out, now!" and with the two RAF police choking on our dust, David pulled smartly away.

As we ate our ices, I wondered if they were likely to try and trace us, but it seemed so unlikely that anything could ever be proved, that we both decided there was no need to worry. What shook us more than anything was to find these police in such an unlikely place at an equally unlikely time. We didn't use the shop again, just in case.

From time to time, another friend, who lived in Norwich, gave me lifts back to camp on a Sunday. He had an old Austin Seven car and was actually stationed at Cranwell. I used to catch the last bus into Norwich at about nine o'clock, getting to his house at around half-past. The car never completely let us down, but it had one or two temperamental parts, particularly the dynamo. It went very steadily but always got us there eventually. The closest we ever came to catastrophe was one very dark, foggy night. Fortunately, there was nothing at all on the roads at the time when we were experiencing our difficulties. The lights became dimmer and dimmer and we had to straddle the cats' eyes in the centre of the road in order to stay on course, straining ears and eyes for other traffic. There was none as, more than once, I had to get out and push. It was after three in the morning when we finally got back, safe, tired and very grubby.

Arranged lifts back were very much a luxury. For three-quarters of the time, I had to rely on bus and train. Last bus up to Norwich, down to Thorpe station for a train journey through the night; that was the usual routine. We ended up in Lincoln at five in the morning, where the TOC H used to open up to give us shelter and sustenance. We would sip tea and talk wearily until it was time to go for the six o'clock bus to Cranwell. This got us to camp at seven, when it was a quick wash and shave, breakfast and to work. Once more I found out how tired I could get because, on such Mondays, I would complete my tasks at flying wing listlessly, perhaps, but effectively. There was never a great deal of flying on Saturday mornings, often there were no forms 79 to deal with at all. This gave me a good opportunity to get my elaborate card index system at headquarters up to date. Up to lunchtime, I would function comparatively normally. In the afternoon, however, after travelling overnight, I would always fall asleep in the middle of the job I was doing. Around three o'clock, I would slump forward on the desk, unable to keep my eyes open any longer. When I first did it, I was both surprised and ashamed, but the friendly civilian (an ex-RAF man himself) who was based in the plans section was most understanding. I felt sure that it wouldn't happen again. But it did, every time. The civilian used to leave me until it was time for him to go home and then he would waken me, with the advice that I should get an early night. The next day, when I returned to the plans section, I would find that my writing had tailed off into a meaningless squiggle on the card I was bringing up to date as I fell asleep.

Very often the trains were crowded on Sundays, full of servicemen travelling to the many RAF stations in Lincolnshire. I would usually meet up with a couple of friends on the platform and, together, we would seek out a comfortable compartment. Not infrequently there was standing room only in the third-class carriages, so we would pop into the first-class section, where we invariably had a compartment to ourselves. Each of us had a flask and sandwiches to tuck into before settling for some sleep. In the end, just for the privacy, we would travel first class anyway, with a third-class ticket, of course. There was never a ticket collector to bother us, but we did once nearly land ourselves in trouble, largely through our own fault.

We had found an empty compartment, settled ourselves for food and drink, and then, as the train was about to depart, we were joined by a fairly distinguished looking stranger. He put his travelling grip on the rack next to mine and took a book from it before settling down to read. No words were exchanged between us, although it was pretty obvious that we were unlikely candidates for first class travel. The three of us finished eating and drinking and, aware only of our own procedure, switched out the lights prior to getting some sleep. The newcomer promptly turned them on again and announced his intentions: -

"I wish to read my book, so I will be obliged if you leave on the lights." There was a note of authority rather than menace in his voice that made us, for the moment, heed his request. Then one of my companions pointed out that there were three of us wishing to sleep and only one of him requiring a light on. It seemed rather undemocratic that the wish of the one should prevail. Good-naturedly, the newcomer agreed to abide by the will of the majority. Before getting my head down for a nap I put my flask back in my bag. Glancing to the right, I saw a folded uniform on the top of the grip next to mine. The tunic was on the top and bore the markings of group captain. No wonder I had detected a note of authority in his voice. I tried to pass on some sort of warning to the others but as I attempted to attract their attention, the group captain had his final say:

"If I decide to read again later on I shall put on the lights again." I was sure he would. I could think of at least two wing commanders, whom he outranked, who would not have been nearly so tolerant. I would have laid odds he was a flying type.

15. GETTING OUT

Because I had been so disappointed to find that West Kirby was not the expected improvement on Padgate, I reserved any judgement on my new base, Cranwell, until I had sampled it. Secretly, however, I felt certain that I had reached rock bottom and that things were bound to get better. And so it proved, almost entirely due to the fact that Cranwell had flying as its central activity. The officers and men attached to the flying wing of the camp were splendid, from the Chief Flying Instructor down to the ordinary erks like myself. I know now that I was extremely fortunate to be given the job of progress clerk, which left me entirely separate from anybody else except a flight lieutenant, with whom I shared a room in the CFI's offices. To begin with, while I was learning the ropes through 'on the job training', my superior was a rather serious, uncommunicative man. This concentrated my mind on the work, which I was taught to do thoroughly. My predecessor had been a commissioned officer, who had been earning a great deal more than the paltry twenty-eight shillings a week that I was being paid.

My main function was to collect the flying returns of the cadets each day and then plot the information gleaned from them on a whole host of charts displayed along the corridor outside the Chief Flying Instructor's office. Included in this was the information concerning the number of aircraft fit to fly each day and the state of the weather. The ultimate purpose of all these charts was to provide the CFI with up-to-date information about the progress of each entry, or class, at the College, so that he could regulate their programme accordingly. All this was then duplicated in my other office in the plans room at the headquarters building of the College, where I would usually go before lunch and for the afternoon. The first CFI that I worked under was a fine chap. I was a little scared of him at the beginning, because he seemed so fierce, but I soon learned that if my work was up to scratch he was all right, and appreciative. The flight lieutenant and I tolerated each other and no more but, after some ten weeks or so, he was posted. His replacement was a man after my own heart and we quickly came to an excellent arrangement. He was interested in flying, at which he excelled, and found the office work boring. All charts and statistics were my province, particularly the weekly statistical return to Flying Training Command which had to be sent off every Friday. Once that was on his desk for signature, then I was free until the morning of the next Monday. He never said as much and, of course, he could not make any spoken agreement to that effect, but he left me to make my own arrangements.

The College worked on a system rather similar to school terms, with the vacations between terms not quite so long, and during these breaks, flying wing would virtually close down. The top cadet entry would graduate and my charts would need adjusting. Once this was done, there wasn't a great deal to do until the cadets began flying again. During the terms, I would work steadily from Monday to Friday, sometimes using part of the evening to keep the new charts up to date, thus leaving myself clear for the holidays. That in itself was not enough. I was fortunate enough to be friendly with the man responsible for the guard roster, who removed my card from the index, so that I wouldn't be posted on orders to do a security patrol. As a secondary precaution, a friend of mine in the billet watched orders in case anything cropped up that required my presence. In case of emergency, he would send me a telegram, to return to camp immediately. It happened but once. Pay parade was changed from Friday to Thursday and he sent off a telegram which had me scrambling back to the camp on the Tuesday evening. That was the only scare.

My father was astonished by the amount of leave I had, because for most of the weeks that the College cadets were on holiday, I would be at home, except for pay day. Of course I needed some luck, getting more than my share of it at times, but it held throughout. For eight consecutive months, I never spent a Saturday or Sunday on camp which, together with the several weeks' holiday I was able to take, allowed me to achieve a near balance of fifty-fifty between civilian and serviceman. Even today I am not at all sure what risks I was taking but I justified what I was doing by the abysmal sum of money I was being paid for doing an officer's job.

The forty people in the same barrack room as myself took the attitude that what I did was my business. Even the corporals turned a blind eye to my prolonged absences. All my friends were clerical staff, either from pay accounts or from the P3 section. (I never did know what P3 stood for). The pay clerks in particular had a tedious job, because they had an officer in charge who required the books to balance exactly, so that, on more than one occasion, the accounts staff from the billet were up practically all night looking for a discrepancy of as little as a penny or two.

Bull nights were on Thursdays, when we had them, but they were not unreasonably frequent. Most evenings we would play bridge or go to the cinema, which changed its programme four times a week. There was always the NAAFI club, of course, but an acute shortage of money used to curtail my visits there. It meant, also, that I could rarely afford the demob parties that almost every airman about to be released would throw. Or perhaps more accurately, would throw up.

A thirty-two-seater coach would be hired to take the revellers off to some nearby pub to say a liquid farewell. The pubs supplied food free of charge and invariably the entire group would return legless. Those of us left in the billet would go downstairs to help those who could not walk unaided. On one occasion there were only four who could make their own way to their beds. One of the drunkest airmen on that occasion wandered across the top of the airfield, quite oblivious of the fact that there was night flying. A small search party eventually found him lying happily in the grass and all returned safely. But getting them to bed was often the easiest part of the operation. Throughout the night, airmen would be sick, and the billet could be a most unpleasant place by morning, especially the wash basins. As if that were not enough, one exuberant airman used to discharge all the large, conical fire extinguishers in the middle of the night. It was an unwritten rule that, whatever the rota, two of the merrymakers would have the task of cleaning up the billet in the morning.

It was most agreeable working amongst the officers and men of the flying wing at Cranwell and it more than compensated for the rather dour nature of those in the headquarters building. I was fortunate in that the only daily contact I had was with a civilian in the plans office. As far as all the comings and goings of officers housed in the building were concerned, I just had to be sure and get my saluting right. From a practical point of view, the beauty of my situation was that if I was not in my room at flying wing, it was assumed I was in my other office and vice versa. Nobody expected me to be in two places at the same time nor, apparently, did they expect me to be in neither.

I suppose that it could not last indefinitely and I could have no complaints about the way in which the balance was partially redressed in my last three months. Guard duties cropped up with some frequency. Only when I had a legitimate forty-eight-hour pass was I able to make an early getaway on a Friday, but by this time it did not seem to matter anymore. I was within sight of getting back to a normal life again. Even my wage had been increased to the astronomical sum of forty-nine shillings a week. All I had to do was go through the motions correctly, teach another man how to do my job and keep out of trouble.

As a going-away present, the sergeant in the flying wing office had me attached to the NAAFI for the Battle of Britain week. This involved humping equipment and provisions round the camp and generally doing all the menial work for the NAAFI as they prepared for this special celebration. There was a bonus in it for me, however, not from the NAAFI, who were incredibly mean to those of us who were allocated all their dirty work, but from the sergeant. A fortnight before I was due to be demobbed, he gave me my clearance chit to be completed: -

"You will not leave this camp until you have obtained all the twenty-two signatures you require from the various sections of the camp. If it's not complete within two weeks then you'll stay until it is."

It sounded simple, but some of the more obscure sections were difficult enough to locate, let alone find the relevant officer to give me the necessary signature. One place I knew well enough was the station sick quarters, where the signature was linked to a satisfactory medical examination. They weighed and measured me, tested my eyes and ears and generally satisfied themselves that I was in good working order. Going through my papers, the MO commented that someone had forgotten to record my vaccination against smallpox. I had in fact never had one.

“I've never been vaccinated, sir", I explained.

"Impossible. No one in the RAF gets through without being vaccinated." I explained how, because my mother had been ill when she was vaccinated as a child, I was not done as a baby. At Padgate I had twice been sent to have the smallpox jab but on both occasions they were out of vaccine. The same had happened at West Kirby and by the time I arrived at Cranwell, it was assumed that I had been vaccinated. The MO knew better. It was not conceivable that I could have gone unnoticed in this way and to avoid any likely delay in my departure I agreed that I must indeed have been vaccinated and the officer signed me off. Several days before the deadline all signatures were in place and I was allowed to leave. With the opposite of a heavy heart but with a weighty case to take home, I set off from the camp for the last time, walking briskly onto the road to King’s Lynn.

I did not look back.